DISASTERS SERIES

MASSACHUSETTS
DISASTERS

TRUE STORIES OF
TRAGEDY AND SURVIVAL

Larry Pletcher

INSIDERS' GUIDE®

GUILFORD, CONNECTICUT
AN IMPRINT OF THE GLOBE PEQUOT PRESS

INSIDERS' GUIDE®

Copyright © 2006 Morris Book Publishing, LLC

Insiders' Guide and TwoDot are registered trademarks of Morris Book Publishing, LLC.

Text design by Pettistudio LLC, www.pettistudio.com
Map by M. A. Dubé © Morris Book Publishing, LLC

Library of Congress Cataloging-in-Publication Data
Pletcher, Larry, 1946-
  Massachusetts disasters : true stories of tragedy and survival / Larry Pletcher. — 1st ed.
      p. cm. — (Disasters series)
  Includes bibliographical references.
  ISBN-13: 978-0-7627-3988-2
  ISBN-10: 0-7627-3988-6
  1. Natural disasters—Massachusetts. 2. Disasters—Massachusetts.
I. Title. II. Series.
  GB5010.P54 2006
  974.4—dc22

                                            2006017418

Manufactured in the United States of America
First Edition/First Printing

Contents

PREFACE

Plowing up the soil of Massachusetts's history allows a writer to toil in very fertile ground. From Plymouth Rock to Bunker Hill to our beloved Fenway Park, this commonwealth in New England boasts a long, proud history and an unusual number of citizens who carry a passion for the past. As a result the history of Massachusetts comes alive not just in buildings and monuments that commemorate the past, but also in the nooks and crannies of libraries and historical societies where the record of that proud past has been meticulously preserved. For a humble writer of history, it just doesn't get any better than that.

New England weather always hides a few surprises. If you don't like the weather, just wait a minute, as the saying goes. Massachusetts also has miles of hazardous coastline and a seafaring tradition. As the centuries have passed, the "hub" of Boston, like many urban areas, has experienced growing pains in adjusting to new modes of transportation. Cities and towns throughout the commonwealth were in the forefront in confronting the challenges of industrialization and urban growth. In selecting chapters for this book, there were plenty of disasters from which to choose.

My overriding goal in presenting these twenty-one stories from Massachusetts's past has been to rely as much as possible on the actual words of the people who survived these harrowing events. The sensibilities and expectations of people who lived one hundred or more years ago were often different from our own. To capture the real flavor of these historic events, I have relied extensively on news reports written at the time. Whether the wreck of the schooner *Eveline Treat* in 1865, the famous molasses flood in 1919, or the hellish Cocoanut Grove fire in 1942, original sources still convey the palpable horror of seamen freezing in the shrouds, workers doomed by flowing goo, and patrons torched by a raging fire.

In poring through thousands of microfilmed pages of newspapers dating back nearly 150 years, I often found it amusing to follow the evolution of the newspapers themselves. When the square-rigger *Maritana* broke apart on Egg Rock in Boston Harbor in 1861, news type was set by hand. Reports in the local papers were short and to the point. News articles of the day looked like little more than intrusions on valuable advertising space, even on the front page. Twenty years later, the editorial approach had changed. Vivid descriptions of suffering and sorrow portray the wreck of a commuter train at Bussey Bridge in West Roxbury, still a rural village in 1887. Sketch artists were even employed to depict the chaos of the train's twisted wreckage at a time before news photographs had yet to come into their own. By 1918 newspapers seemed willing to print just about anything and everything that came into their hands. Rambling eyewitness accounts of a German submarine firing at Cape Cod during the "Battle of Orleans" were printed at length—even if they were sometimes pointless and inconsistent. Photographs of the day's heroes were prominently displayed—even if the blurry images were often a little hard to decipher.

Of course some things never change. Carelessness is always with us. The needless loss of life on Martha's Vineyard's wave-swept rocks survives in history as an object lesson in how not to sail a ship. The collision of trains at a station in Revere in 1871 bears an eerie resemblance to the spectacular crash of an Amtrak and commuter train at Back Bay station in 1990.

Greed and avarice never go away. The urge to cut corners echoes through any list of man-made mayhem—locking fire doors to control access to a nightclub, building a shoddy dam, failing to maintain an oil tanker, and pouring concrete in freezing weather have all lead to major Massachusetts disasters.

Happily, a resourceful human spirit is also a timeless constant. The plucky resolve of passengers stranded in railroad cars during the blizzard of 1888 surfaces again in the good-natured response of urban motorists caught in a record-breaking storm ninety years later. Through tornado, hurricane, fire and flood, these stories of heroic deeds prove that selfless courage will find a way to prevail—a comforting thought in a world in which unheard-of disasters certainly lay ahead.

I would like to thank Mike Urban, Amy Paradysz, and Dan Spinella for introducing me to this project, editing the manuscript, and polishing the work. Special thanks as well to the Boston Public Library, the staff of its microfilm department, and the citizens of Massachusetts who support their efforts.

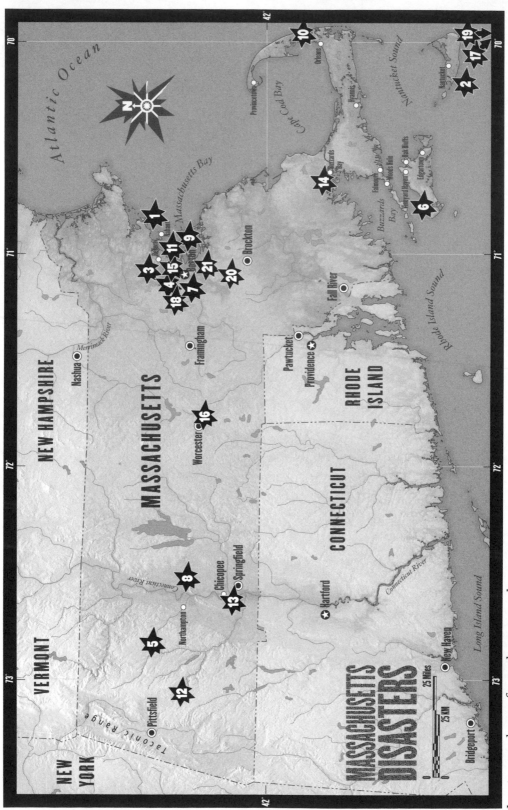

Locator numbers refer to chapter numbers.

CHAPTER 1

BOSTON HARBOR'S WORST SHIPWRECK

The Sinking of the *Maritana*

1861

In the days before interstate highways and long-distance rail-roads, coastal waterways were America's lifeline of trade. Square-rigged sailing ships connected East Coast ports to Europe and the West Indies. Smaller schooners and barques by the hundreds linked Boston with Providence, New York, New Haven, Philadelphia, and Savannah. Each day, food, fuel, iron, and fiber entered Massachusetts ports to furnish the people of New England with the necessities of life.

But navigation along the East Coast was a hazardous business, and no area was more hazardous than the coast of Massachusetts. From the shoals off Nantucket Island, to the currents and rips of Cape Cod, to the outcrops of rock that ring Boston Harbor, guiding a vessel to safe harbor was a risky business. Well over a thousand ships, large and small, have come to a tragic end off the Massachusetts coast.

As early as 1715 the Massachusetts legislature voted to build a lighthouse on Little Brewster Island to guide ships into

Boston Harbor. More lighthouses would follow over the years, but shipwrecks continued to occur regularly. The beaches of Cape Cod and Nantasket were often awash with cargo and debris of unfortunate ships that were lost offshore. "Wreckers" in these areas conducted a lucrative business in salvaging these cargoes, sometimes doing so even before the ships had completely broken up or sunk.

Not only cargoes but human beings also washed ashore. Fortunately, other citizens of Massachusetts were more compassionate than the wreckers. As a result, in 1786 the Humane Society of the Commonwealth of Massachusetts (better known as the Massachusetts Humane Society) was organized. Its purpose back then was not to shelter stray dogs and cats, but rather: "For the recovery of persons who meet with such accidents as to produce in them the appearance of death, and for promoting the cause of humanity by pursuing such means from time to time as shall have for their object the preservation of human life and the alleviation of its miseries."

None other than Paul Revere and Samuel Adams were members of the Massachusetts Humane Society, which naturally focused its attention on trying to aid the survivors of shipwrecks. The society soon built a series of huts, or Charity Houses, on isolated beaches in the state. Crudely outfitted with kindling, food, and a bit of hay to sleep on, the huts were meant to keep a body alive if washed ashore on a stormy night.

By 1840 the Humane Society progressed to providing lifeboats in addition to huts. Now with the aid of volunteers, the society could take an active role in trying to save the lives of shipwreck victims. One of the first sites for a hut and lifeboat station was near Hull at Point Allerton at the far end of Nantasket Beach. Overlooking the main outcrop-strewn entrance to Boston Harbor, the lifesaving volunteers in the area were assured an active business. Rescues by the men of Hull became synonymous with bravery and courage in the face of an angry sea.

The *Maritana*, a 991-ton sailing ship built in Quincy in 1857, was designed to haul cargo across the Atlantic. At its bow stood a graceful hand-carved figurehead that had first appeared on the French ship *Berceau*, which had been captured in the war of 1798. The carving later found its way onto the bow of the American ship *Caroline*, which sank off the coast of Nantucket. Finally, owners from Providence chose the star-crossed figurehead to grace the bow of the *Maritana*, which would soon provide the men of Hull with one of their most famous rescues.

The *Maritana* sailed from Liverpool, England, on September 25, 1861, bound for Boston with fourteen passengers and a hold filled with coal, wool, potash, steel, and iron. It was not an easy trip. The ship encountered rough weather during the entire passage, including several severe gales that damaged her rigging and ripped her sails. Still, Capt. G. W. Williams, of Dedham, knew his trade and took pride in his craft. With several days to go before reaching the American coast, the crew was put to work painting the woodwork, scraping the decks, polishing the brass, and putting the ship in proper trim.

At 4:30 P.M. on Saturday, November 2, 1861, the ship passed Highland Light on the upper arm of Cape Cod. Fair weather seemed to promise a happy homecoming as the ship approached its destination. By 8:45 P.M., with the dangers of the Cape mostly behind them, the *Maritana* passed

Race Light at Provincetown with the seas now in a heavy flood tide.

As the ship worked its way north up the coast and made Minot Light on the shore near Scituate, the wind increased and the clouds grew heavy. Like the rest of the voyage, the homecoming would not be simply routine. All hands were called on deck to shorten sail in what was now a heavy blow.

The weather thickened as the ship approached the harbor. In heavy rain and fog, the *Maritana* ran briskly before the wind. The crew strained to see Boston Light, a beacon that would guide them through the rocky outcrops and small islands that ringed the outer harbor.

Finally, in the pitch dark of 12:45 A.M. Sunday, the lookout spotted the welcome light. But the same moment also revealed the deadly sight of the bright white foam of ocean breakers. Captain Williams shouted the order for the helmsman to turn hard up into the wind, but the order came too late. In a high tide the *Maritana* was driven sideways into the boulder spikes of Egg Rock, a barren ledge jutting barely above water about a half mile east of Boston Light.

The *Maritana* was a sturdy ship. Caught amidships, the vessel endured the pounding of the waves and the grinding of its wooden hull on the pointed pinnacles of rock. At high tide the rugged vessel might have survived, but the passing hours brought a falling tide. As the water level retreated, more and more of the ship's weight was carried by the midpoint of the hull where the ship was fatally caught. It was just a matter of time before the final disaster.

To ease the strain on his listing ship, at 3 A.M. the captain ordered the crew to cut down the masts. Again ill-fortune paid a visit. As the mizzenmast fell it struck and stove in a lifeboat.

Crew and passengers could do little but sound the ship's bell as a signal of distress and pray that the ship would hold together until dawn.

With first light a signal flag flying from Boston Light told the crew that the lighthouse keeper knew of their peril, but their circumstances grew increasingly desperate. In the high seas of a northeast storm, five seamen clambered into a lifeboat in an attempt to get a line to the relative safety of the barren rock. If they could fasten a rope to a pinnacle, they might be able to save the passengers. In short order the lifeboat was swamped by waves as the fury of the gale persisted. All five men clung to the small boat as the rest of the crew hauled on a line to drag it back to the ship.

A hero was needed, and a seaman named Thomas Haney volunteered. The *Boston Daily Journal* described his ordeal:

> Thomas Haney then fastened a life preserver to his body and springing into the sea, with a line attached, struck out for the shore. He reached the rock, over which the sea broke with great violence, prostrating the man, and compelling his companions to draw him back to the vessel. He reached the deck more dead than alive.

What now? Was there a way for the crew to save themselves and their passengers? A few members of the crew dragged out the gangplank and used it as a makeshift raft to try to land on Egg Rock. Again, a valiant effort, but again the men were defeated and hauled back to the ship. The second mate, James Donnough, was next to try. A good swimmer, Donnough tied a lead line to his body and dove into the sea. Again, the crashing surf proved stronger than the man.

As the tide continued to fall, it was clear to Captain Williams that the end of the ship was near. The passengers were called on deck and final preparations were begun. Passengers and crew were ordered into the weather chains. Criss-crossing the deck and securely fastened, the chains were the last desperate attempt to prolong life on a storm-tossed ship.

About half of the passengers were directed toward the bow and half to the roof of the pilothouse in the stern. Struggling to reach their assigned positions in the steady gale, a woman and her daughter were struck by a heavy sea and washed overboard to their deaths.

No sooner had the passengers secured themselves than the dreaded event occurred. At about 8 A.M., the crashing surf claimed its victory and the *Maritana* broke in two. As the ship disintegrated, cargo began floating out of the hull, and Captain Williams fell into a chasm that opened on the quarterdeck. "Look out for yourselves!" the captain shouted according to one account, but the ship's carpenter tells a different tale: "He went down between the broken fragments, which closing suddenly caught the Captain by the head and crushed it in a frightful manner. Another sea opened the gap and Mr. Carnes, the mate, lifted the lifeless body of the Captain to the deck."

As the ship broke apart, the forward half of the vessel was quickly swept under the waves, and all passengers and crew who clung to the unlucky portion were immediately drowned. Seven fortunate survivors in the stern were saved when the roof of the pilothouse broke loose and floated them to the safety of Egg Rock. Pounded against the rock, survivors suffered only severe bruises and in one case a broken nose.

According to the *Boston Evening Transcript,* "Five others swam ashore. One poor fellow, after reaching the rock in safety, was swept back to the ship by a heavy sea which stunned him; but, while he lay insensible, another wave returned him to the rock, where he was finally rescued."

Seldom are people desperate enough to consider themselves lucky to huddle on a wave-washed rock in a bitter November gale. Two passengers and eleven members of the crew had escaped the shattered ship, but their survival was still in question.

Moses Barrett, the keeper of Boston Light, had lost sight of the lights of the *Maritana* in the middle of the night. With dawn on Sunday pieces of cargo and bits of hull washed up on the beach confirmed his worst fears. When the storm began to lift at midday, Barrett was able to see the remains of the ship, but he knew that his small lifeboat was no match for the breakers. Because of the heavy seas, the survivors shivered on Egg Rock until 2 P.M., when Barrett's signal flag drew a response from the pilot boat *William Sharkey* and the volunteers of Hull.

In tossing seas the skilled rescuers set to work. Launching two small dories from the pilot boat, the lifesavers threw a line to the survivors huddled on the rock. With the line secured to a pinnacle, one of the dories then made fast the other end, stretched the line taught, and laid offshore. With the aid of the taught line, the second dory, with Samuel James at the helm, inched its way toward the rocks. One by one the survivors leaped into the dory and were finally saved.

Capt. Samuel James, of Hull, was the son of William James, and the brother of Joshua James. All three contributed greatly to the gallant reputation of the lifesavers of Hull. Joshua James later became the most famous member of the United

States Life-Saving Service. For their efforts in the rescue of the *Maritana*, Samuel James, together with H. S. Locke and George Kibble, received a certificate from the humane society for "Heroism in Boston Bay," along with the usual award of ten dollars.

Eleven crew members and thirteen passengers died in the wreck of the *Maritana*, which became known as the worst in the history of Boston Harbor. Bodies, pieces of cargo, and "relics" washed ashore for weeks after the disaster. Letters from Captain William's children, a purse with eight and a half sovereigns, and a finger ring were returned to the captain's widow.

A few days after the sinking, the figurehead from the ship was salvaged and brought to Lincoln Wharf. The wharf later caught fire, and the figurehead never returned to sea.

CHAPTER 2

ONE MAN'S COURAGE

The Wreck of the *Eveline Treat*

1865

Sometimes, it's not the magnitude of the disaster but the sheer courage of the rescue that earns an event a spot in the pages of history.

The sailing ship *Eveline Treat* was wholly unremarkable. A small coastal schooner with a captain and four-man crew, the *Eveline Treat* hauled coal along the Atlantic coast. Going about its daily business, it was just one of hundreds of working ships that carried cargo for a young nation. As is the case with a tractor-trailer on a modern interstate highway, a mishap involving such a carrier would have to be truly spectacular to merit public attention.

There was nothing really remarkable about the disaster that befell the *Eveline Treat* in 1865. Making its way from Philadelphia to Gloucester, the fore-and-aft schooner from Maine found itself rounding Nantucket Island on a Friday night in heavy seas and a fresh wind. Either Capt. Job Philbrook or one of his crew made an error in navigation. Mistaking Sankaty Light for Gay Head, the vessel struck the rocks of Miacomet Rip, on the south side of the island near the entrance to Miacomet Pond. Grinding to a halt at about midnight, the *Eveline Treat* was just another ship gone aground on the rocky shoals off Nantucket.

Massachusetts newspapers eventually carried the story. Three days after the grounding, the *Boston Post* included the news from Nantucket along with brief accounts of ten other ships off the northeast coast that had gone aground, sprung leaks, or otherwise wrecked. The following paragraph is the entire *Post* story:

> A fore and aft schooner, name unknown, is ashore in the breakers, South side of the island, and will probably be a total loss. The crew are in the rigging. Assistance has gone to them, and they will probably be saved.

The *Boston Herald* included a full paragraph about the wreck tucked between accounts of an execution and a suicide. More space was devoted to news about a crewman who was lost at sea. Even a story about a ship's captain who fell off the dock into the harbor was apparently more newsworthy in Boston.

A day earlier than the Boston papers, the *New Bedford Daily Evening Standard* was even more succinct.

> Nantucket, Oct. 21—There is a schooner in the breakers outside this harbor. The crew, who are in the rigging, will be saved, but the vessel will probably go to pieces.

While the big city newspapers found the small wreck off Nantucket barely newsworthy, Captain Philbrook, his two sons, and two other crewmen clearly saw the wreck from a different perspective. Their lives were at stake. Their circumstances were dire. For them the disaster was anything but routine. Fortunately for captain and crew, the people of Nantucket shared their more urgent views.

The imperiled ship was first discovered with the light of dawn on Saturday morning. Caught on the rocks about 300 yards from shore, the vessel was pummeled by strong winds and a heavy surf that sent a constant procession of waves breaking over its deck. The captain and crew had already endured the frigid pounding of the breakers for several hours. They were helpless to save the ship. The men were rapidly reaching a point of exhaustion that would leave them helpless to save their own lives.

The vessel was in immediate danger of breaking up, and its tiny deckhouse was being beaten by crashing waves. The boiling surf between ship and shore would swamp any lifeboat and drown a desperate man trying to swim. The crew was down to the coastal sailor's last chance if not for survival then at least for a little more time—they lashed themselves to the rigging. Climbing above the deck and above the crashing sea, captain and crew tied themselves onto the strong lines that held the mast in place. Wet, cold, tired, and afraid, they waited for dawn. They watched as the angry ocean tore the deckhouse off the ship and washed it away.

Nantucket Islanders were seafaring people familiar with the perils of rock and surf. They understood the need for a prompt response. They had done this sort of rescue before. Volunteers from the local brigade of the Massachusetts Humane Society were alerted to the problem and the appropriate equipment was brought to the beach.

Fierce wind and surf made a lifeboat rescue out of the question, so Capt. Joseph Hamblin and Joseph Perry placed a howitzer or mortar in position under the direction of Captain Barney. A thin line was fired over the bow of the stricken vessel. The thin line was then used to haul a heavier rope or hawser out to the ship—a virtual lifeline to connect ship to shore.

The *Nantucket Inquirer and Mirror* described the beginning of this rescue attempt: "A small line was fired over the disabled vessel, and luckily secured by the captain's son, who, although stiff and cold from exposure, worked with commendable energy, and succeeded in hauling the hawser across, making it fast to the masthead."

All that was required now was for a sling seat or life-sling to be attached to the hawser, and one after another the captain and crew could be hauled ashore. At this point, though, with successful rescue in sight, bad luck intervened.

Captain Philbrook himself was tied lower down in the rigging than the rest of the crew. He was sixty-two, an age that the newspapers seemed to imply was a bit too old for the task at hand. One of his sons tried to help him into the sling. The *Nantucket Inquirer and Mirror* again described the scene: "In vain were the efforts of the gallant son to prevail upon his father to get into the life-sling. The old weather-beaten captain made the attempt; but his courage failing him, he resumed his former place in the shrouds, and refused to move."

Roaring wind and rough seas made communication between the rescuers and crew impossible. As crowds gathered along the shore, the rescue effort seemed to have stalled until the mate of the *Eveline Treat* decided it was time to act. Releasing the lines that lashed him to the rigging, he fastened himself into the sling seat and prepared for the crossing to shore.

Engraving of a shipwreck, possibly the Essex, *from the era of the* Eveline Treat.
COURTESY OF THE NANTUCKET HISTORICAL ASSOCIATION, F6770

Volunteers on the beach pulled the life-sling along a stout, heavy rope called a hawser above the waves toward shore. But part way across, the action of wind and waves snarled one of the ropes. The sling was stuck and the mate suspended above the sea. Fortunately, he was close enough to shore that people on the beach were able to throw him another line. Tying the line to his waist, the mate freed himself from the sling and fell into the sea. Islanders dragged the man ashore, frigid but alive.

One of the captain's sons was next. Drenched and beaten by waves, he was eventually rescued in a slow, time-consuming process. By now, though, the daylight of late October was quickly fading and the elderly captain was still lashed to the rigging of the foundering ship.

The people of Nantucket knew they were running out of time. The rescue team attached a life-car, sturdier than a sling, to the stout hawser that stretched to the ship. Daniel Folger then volunteered to ride the life-car out to the stricken vessel in a last-ditch effort to convince the captain to climb into the car and put his fate in the rescuer's hands. But the life-car failed to work.

Now late in the afternoon, the captain's second son and the sailors still on the ship were able to coax the captain out of the rigging. After helping the captain into a sling seat, they firmly tied him in to keep him safe. With sympathy for the frailty of their trussed and bound passenger, rescue personnel on shore pulled on the ropes with all their might to draw the captain toward land.

The *Nantucket Inquirer and Mirror* continued the rescue story:

> When mid-way between the vessel and the beach, the line became entangled in the hands of the men in the rigging, and for an hour and a half, perhaps, the captain hung, swinging over a yawning surge, wet and cold. The men in the shrouds, still worked upon the snarled rope, with a Trojan's will; but it would not give way. Still there was the captain, hanging upon the hawser, with head uncovered, cramped from the nature of his position, with the drifting sea-foam beating his face, and drenching him to the skin. What was to be done? Who was the man for the hour? Was he there?

Three lives literally hung in the balance. Not only was the captain in danger of dying from exposure as he was splashed by the angry sea, but the two sailors still out on the ship were now stranded without a clear path to shore.

Extraordinary conditions often compel extraordinary responses. Frederick W. Ramsdell, a Nantucket man with a robust build, stood on the dank shore and saw the need for immediate action. With the confidence of youth, Ramsdell grabbed a knife, held the knife in his mouth, and tied a rope around his waist. The crowd on the beach looked on with fear and hope as Ramsdell sprang onto the hawser and began to inch his way out toward the desperate captain.

Slowly, through windswept foam and breaking waves, Ramsdell climbed hand over hand along the hawser suspended above the turbulent ocean for more than 100 yards. When he reached the captain, Ramsdell perched on the bobbing hawser and cut the snarled lines where they were attached to the life-sling. Removing the line from his waist, he then tied that line to the sling so that rescuers could pull the sling toward shore.

Cold and wet, and strained by the exertion, Ramsdell now faced the return trip to the beach without the safety of a line around his waist. Friends on shore no longer held a rope that could save him by dragging him back to the beach. One slip from the soggy hawser would send him to a watery grave. Hand over hand, hanging below the thick hawser, he passed through the misery inflicted by wind and wave. Late on that cold October afternoon, Frederick Ramsdell stepped onto the beach a hero.

With a new line attached, the rescue of the captain was quickly completed. Eager hands hauled him the remaining yards to shore. Close to death, he was whisked away in a waiting carriage and taken to a nearby home for the healing effects of hot food and a warm fire.

While the captain recuperated, a final line was spliced into place on the running block and the sling returned to the ship. Without further delay the remaining men of the crew were drawn to safety along the hawser. Though the crowds on the beach returned to their homes, it was not just another day on Nantucket Island.

The *Nantucket Inquirer and Mirror* foresaw the timeless appeal of the day's events:

> Darkness crept on apace; but the lights around every fireside burned brighter that night, and eyes opened wider, at the thrilling story of five men who were rescued from a watery grave. God was thanked, and the brave man remembered, who risked his own life that three men might live. It will be a long time before that day's deeds will be forgotten.

For his efforts Frederick Ramsdell was recognized with a silver medal, the Massachusetts Humane Society's highest award.

THE GREAT REVERE DISASTER

Crash on the Eastern Railroad

1871

The dog days of summer. Hot suffocating air with barely a breeze stirring. Ocean mist drifting inland fogging the North Shore. August 26, 1871, brought weather that shortens the temper, tests the patience, and leads to error.

People found plenty of reasons to get out of Boston on that steamy Saturday night. Mary Ann Crowley was determined to stay over in Beverly and go to a camp meeting in Hamilton on Monday morning. Charles Story, his wife, and young daughter were simply getting away to Beverly to visit friends. Rev. Dr. Ezra Gannett of the Arlington Street Unitarian Church was on his way to Lynn to preach a sermon as a visiting minister.

Near chaos reigned at the Eastern Railroad terminal in Boston as crowds of businessmen and families descended on the station anxious to get out of town. As usual on the Eastern, trains were running late, but the confusion on this summer Saturday evening seemed even worse than passengers had come to expect.

Aside from large crowds, delays on the Eastern were often caused by the company's track system and rules of the road north of Boston. The main-line track that ran from Boston through Revere and on to Beverly carried the Beverly local or "accommodation" train as well as the main-line Portland express or "Pullman" train. In addition that same main-line track also carried Saugus local trains as far as the Saugus Branch that departed the main line south of Revere.

Problems arose when southbound Saugus trains were late or delayed. Rules of the railroad prohibited any northbound train from proceeding from the main line onto the Saugus Branch until southbound trains from the Saugus Branch had passed by and cleared.

On that night in Boston, Jeremiah Prescott, superintendent of the Eastern Railroad, had more than his usual share of problems. Engine trouble had delayed a southbound local train in Saugus. A northbound Saugus train could not proceed and was blocking the entire main line. Short-tempered crowds were gathering in the Eastern Railroad's Boston station, and the trains were running late.

As he waited for railroad cars to complete his train, John S. Noland, conductor of the Beverly accommodation train was told by depot master Hunt that Prescott "was very anxious to have the train start." Three coaches were filled with passengers who jammed the platforms at the front and back of each car and stood packed in the aisles. The Beverly local left Boston at about 7:45 P.M., more than half an hour late. Conductor Noland knew that the Portland express was scheduled to leave on the same track at 8 P.M., but Noland wasn't worried:

The fact that there were but a few minutes between me and the following train did not alarm me. . . . When I went out of the depot, I supposed that the depot master or the superintendent would notify the other train as to where I was.

Noland was almost right. As the Portland express was about to leave the station, Prescott grew concerned about the crowded northbound track. He summoned depot master Hunt.

"The Beverly accommodation train left ten minutes late."

"Yes, sir," replied Hunt.

"Then tell Brown [the engineer of the Portland express] to look out and not run into it."

Hunt later confirmed that the message had been delivered, but the message that William O. Brown received was only to "be on the watch" for trains ahead of him. Brown, of course, didn't need a message to know that! Engineers were always responsible to keep watch ahead of them. What Brown wasn't told was that the Beverly train had departed the Eastern terminal only a little more than ten minutes ahead of him.

One other chance event then occurred that sealed the fate of twenty-nine passengers. A Saugus branch local that was scheduled to leave Boston nearly an hour before the other trains left the station between the Beverly and Portland trains. What seemed to be a harmless third train sandwiched between the accommodation and Pullman trains set the stage for a fatal disaster.

On its way at last, the Beverly accommodation train was delayed for a few minutes at its first stop in Somerville. The

THE DANGER SIGNAL.

The Courier and Ives print "The Danger Signal," created in 1884, depicts an engineer of a locomotive giving a danger signal as another train approaches, much as happened on the Eastern Railroad.
LIBRARY OF CONGRESS, PRINTS & PHOTOGRAPHS DIVISION, LC-USZC4-3155

passengers who weren't annoyed already started to get nervous. A handful of concerned customers even decided to get off the train before the Beverly local continued north to the bottleneck near the junction with the Saugus branch.

Arriving at the junction, the Beverly train gave a blast on its whistle and stopped behind another train. Following the rules of the road, Noland, the conductor, and his brakeman hopped off the back of the Beverly local. He told the *Boston Herald:*

My brakeman started back with a lantern and I followed him; a short distance back we saw a train, signaled it, and it stopped; then we returned to my train;

we took on another engine here and then proceeded having been delayed at the junction about eight minutes.

As the Beverly train continued on to its next stop in Everett, Noland was no longer overly concerned about delays. According to his calculations, his train was running ahead of the express, which would not overtake them. Besides, the express had not been in sight when he flagged down the Saugus train that came up behind them at the Saugus junction. But the fact that Noland didn't see the Portland express didn't mean it wasn't there. Unknown to Noland, the express had already reached the Saugus junction and was hidden behind the Saugus train.

Onboard the Portland express, engineer Brown had sounded his whistle and stopped at the Saugus junction, just as the train ahead of him was getting under way. When the Saugus local in front of him quickly turned off onto the Saugus branch, Brown saw only clear track ahead. In the rolling mist of a summer night, he saw no sign of the two white lanterns that hung on the back of the Beverly train. It was time to pour on steam and resume the journey north.

The Beverly train was scheduled to stop in Revere for only a minute or so. Jumping off the rear car, conductor Noland looked back down the track and yelled out "All right!" and the stationmaster said the same. The accommodation train had been stopped for less than forty-five seconds when another shout rang out. As Noland later recalled it at a coroner's inquest, as reported by the *Boston Daily Evening Transcript:*

I can't say whether the train had started or not when someone cried "The train is coming!" I sprang out on the track and swung my lantern five or six times and another man with a lantern did the same. I then jumped for my life and was not more than fifteen feet away when the crash came.

Estimates of the speed of the express differed greatly—depending on who was asked. The brakeman on the express thought his train was only going 10 miles per hour; a passenger on the express estimated 40 miles per hour. Survivors on the Beverly train said the express was going full speed—as high as 85 miles per hour.

The *Boston Post* best described the scene:

The iron monster rushed over the rails with lightning velocity. Its dazzling head-light flung a sheet of flame over the path of destruction. It swayed back and forth in its eagerness for the crash. Noland was too late. He signaled in vain. There was no hope now. All was lost.

Survivors remember the shriek of the whistle of the speeding train sounding almost together with the noise of the impact, but memories of such events are often faulty. After sounding the alarm, the engineer of the Portland express knew that there was no hope of stopping his train. He set the brakes, threw the locomotive into reverse without letting out steam, and simply dove out the door. The fireman on the locomotive watched the bizarre actions of his engineer and knew what to do. Without stopping to ask why, he also threw himself out the door and saved his own life.

The steaming Portland locomotive blasted into the passenger coach at the rear of the Beverly train and telescoped the car to about one-third of its normal length. About twelve passengers died as a result of the horrible impact as the locomotive literally burrowed itself into the passenger coach. Again the *Boston Post* provided a description:

> It jammed and bruised and mangled and tore and disfigured beyond recognition a dozen of those who a moment before had been in the full enjoyment of life and health. It demolished itself in its mad fury, leaving at the end of the car its smokestack and cab and whistle, and then it stopped, piston rods bent, cylinders broken, trucks gone.

The impact was devastating, but the worst was yet to come as the horror continued—in slow motion. When the locomotive buried itself in the passenger car, the car's roof and sidewalls remained intact. Bad luck. Along with trapped survivors, the passenger car now contained the steaming boiler of a powerful locomotive. The boiler sprang a leak. Billowing clouds of scalding steam crept through the wrecked car.

Mary Crowley and her companion, a Miss Foley, survived the initial impact and didn't feel much of a jolt. Bewildered, they watched for a few seconds as passengers rushed from the car in panic. Mary and her friend were about to leave too when the deadly billows struck. As scalding clouds of steam wafted over them, Mary Crowley screamed and fatally scorched her lungs. Miss Foley was fortunate enough to carry a raincoat and possessed the presence of mind to place it over her face.

When Mary's brother was summoned to the Boston City Hospital, she knew that she "was going fast." The *Boston Herald* described her condition:

> Her face was terribly scalded and the skin peeled off. Her hands were badly scalded and swollen, and she spoke with great difficulty . . . she was injured internally, the coating of her lungs being scalded. She remained conscious long enough to see her mother and give some general instructions for her burial.

Although injured, Mary's companion, Miss Foley, survived.

A Mr. Goodwin of Lynn was horrified by the flash of the Portland express's headlight an instant before he was knocked to the floor of the passenger car. Jammed between seats with another man lying prone at his feet and the mutilated body of a woman on top of him, Goodwin could only look up to the locomotive looming above him. Before a jet of steam could reach his face, he located his hat, which had fallen within reach. Clapping his hat over his face, Goodwin awaited rescue.

Several passengers survived through sheer dumb luck. An impatient young man who was leaning out the window at the time of the wreck was simply ejected and landed beside the tracks. Another, lying beneath the rear wheels of the locomotive, regained consciousness completely unhurt. For Willie Stocker there was both good news and bad. The *Boston Daily Evening Transcript* described his predicament:

> He was thrown down in a half-sitting position with his head bowed slightly, and on his head a very fleshy

woman was seated. The woman was incapable of shifting her position, being insensible and terribly cut about the head. Her weight resting on young Stocker's bowed head soon became intolerable, and as his hands were free he held his burden up with them as long as his strength allowed. Then his head relieved his hands, and thus alternating, the unfortunate youth passed the time of his embarrassing confinement.

News of the crash spread quickly. William Harris, Col. T. L. Porter, Charles Bird, the town clerk, a Mr. Hall, and other prominent citizens of Revere immediately came to the scene to begin rescue. Again, according to the *Transcript:*

No time was to be lost, and orders were immediately issued to tear off the sides of the rear car and release those who were confined therein. All this time the shrieks and groans of the wounded were terrible to hear . . . strong ropes were procured, and after almost superhuman effort the sides of the car were pulled off and the interior revealed.

At the instant of the crash, one young man from Lynn had been thrown to the ceiling of the passenger car. Wedged between the ceiling and the top of the locomotive, he was unable to move until rescue work began. When the sides of the car were torn away, the young man rolled out and fell to the ground. His only injuries, which were minor, were the results of the fall.

The fatalities in the spectacular wreck occurred in the last car of the Beverly local, but passengers in two other cars were not completely spared. Seated in the first of the three passenger coaches, Charles Story felt what he described to the *Boston Daily Evening Transcript* as a long, grinding crash; saw passengers thrown into the aisle; and felt his daughter torn out of his arms.

> Instantaneous with the first sensation, the lights were extinguished, and inside the cars it was total darkness; someone called out, "The danger is all over—don't be afraid!" The passengers were all trampling over one another in their fright and excitement . . . the next instant a man near the rear door shouted, "The car is on fire!" and the excitement was fiercer than ever.

The Story family escaped as kerosene spilled out of lanterns and set the upholstery and wooden paneling on fire in the forward cars. Rescue workers pushed the flaming remains of the Beverly train farther up the track, allowing the fires to burn themselves out. Others joined in the gruesome task of pulling the dead and dying from the steam-scorched rear car.

The majority of twenty-nine deaths and fifty-seven injuries were caused by the locomotive's scalding steam. Here's how the *Transcript* described the macabre results:

> Some of the bodies were swollen to twice their natural size from the effects of the steam, and in some places the flesh upon the exposed places was so thoroughly cooked that upon being roughly touched it detached itself from the bones. In one instance the entire flesh upon a hand of one of the victims came off like a glove, leaving the bones white and bare.

As fatalities were loaded onto a railcar for transport back to Boston, friends and relatives found it difficult to identify the victims. Worshippers in Lynn wondered why Reverend Gannett failed to appear to deliver his guest sermon on Sunday morning. Back in Revere, his body was not identified until later in the day.

Anger over the cavalier attitude of the Eastern Railroad surfaced with a vengeance within twenty-four hours of the accident. Huge crowds gathered to hear speakers blame the disaster not on "the mysterious providence of God, but the reckless carelessness of man."

Even though telegraph lines followed the railroad tracks north to Portland, Superintendent Prescott of the Eastern Railroad didn't believe in such newfangled inventions. Kerosene lanterns, signal lights, and face-to-face contact had been used since railroads began. The old methods had incurred little expense.

The Great Revere Disaster is credited with creating a new public mood in which corporate indifference would not be tolerated. In public rallies throughout Massachusetts, resolutions demanded use of the telegraph so that railroad engineers could not leave a station without receipt of an actual message that said that the road ahead was clear. For railroads in New England, August 26, 1871 was the dawn of a new era.

WHOLESALE RUIN

The Great Boston Fire
1872

In the gaslight era public transportation in the city of Boston was supplied by horse-railways. With jangling bells and clip-clopping hooves, the horse-drawn cars of the Metropolitan, Cambridge, Middlesex, Broadway, and Highland lines carried Bostonians throughout a city that boasted many of the landmarks that we love today. Dignified Beacon Hill rose above Boston Common and the Public Garden. Historic Faneuil Hall, the Old South Meeting House, and the Old State House stood proudly in the heart of the city, and the steeple of the Old North Church soared in the North End as it had in the days of Paul Revere.

But in the fall of 1872, most of the horses in Boston became sick with distemper. Without teams to pull them, the familiar sounds of the horse-railways fell silent. Because of the illness, Boston's fire department lacked horses too. Without teams to pull them, Boston's new steam-engine pumpers had to reach fires the old-fashioned way. Residents chuckled at the sight of breathless firemen tugging on ropes to pull their shining equipment through city streets. Few imagined that heroic efforts by the entire Boston Fire Department, twenty-eight engine companies from eighteen neighboring Massachusetts towns, and nine units from three other New England states would soon be required to save Boston's beloved landmarks.

The evening of November 9, 1872, was a pleasant one in Boston. Saturday night shoppers wandered from store to store. Theatergoers flocked downtown, and strollers filled the city streets merely to enjoy the unseasonably mild temperature.

Soon, though, a large crowd gathered on Washington Street and craned their necks for a look down Summer Street. Far down the length of this narrow thoroughfare, spectators spied glowing billows of smoke pouring from the top of a mansard roof. "Has the alarm been given?" a night clerk asked. "Yes" came a shout from the crowd.

"But where are the firemen?" pedestrians idly grumbled as they resumed their evening strolls.

Across the river in Charlestown, two policemen watched a drawbridge close and checked the time on their watches. With a glance toward Boston, they noted the glow of a fire in the city. It was 7:08 P.M.

Officer Page of the Boston Police Department was walking north on Lincoln Street when he heard the shouts of spectators and saw a nearby glow. Hurrying to the corner of Bedford Street about a block away from the fire, Page made the first call to the fire department when he opened alarm box 52 and sounded the alarm.

At City Hall the alarm operator relayed the news to fire-houses throughout the city and then recorded the time. It was 7:24! Incredibly, a fire visible from as far away as Charlestown had raged in the heart of Boston for at least fifteen minutes before firefighters were informed. The delay would prove calamitous.

Box 52 stood near the edge of Boston's wholesale district. To the north and east of this business zone were the historic landmarks at the city's core. To the south was Boston harbor and the city's docks. The *Boston Daily Advertiser* set the scene this way:

> Here was the centre of the leading market of the country for American dry goods. Here also, a little farther to the east, and also in the path of the fire, was the great boot and shoe market of the world . . . the magnificent wholesale blocks on Summer Street, the dry goods commission houses on Franklin, Summer, and Devonshire streets . . . the wholesale wool houses and the paper dealers on Federal street, the great leather warehouses on Pearl street, the clothing establishments of Arch and Devonshire streets and Otis place, the stations of the Hartford and Erie Railroad and hundreds of smaller stores.

Boston's wholesale area was a warren of narrow streets lined with tall granite or brick buildings topped with high mansard roofs. First settled as a residential zone of family homes with shady yards, the mercantile district in Boston had literally outgrown the city's ability to extinguish fires. Water mains were undersized and rusty, and water pressure in the district was low. Chief engineer John S. Damrell, head of the Boston Fire Department, knew that a prompt, massive response was needed for any alarm sounded from box 52.

A new five-story granite building stood on the corner of Kingston and Summer Streets. According to the *Advertiser*, "The lower floor and basement were occupied by Messrs. Tebbetts, Baldwin & Davis wholesale dry-goods dealers; the second and third stories by Damon, Temple & Co., dealers in hosiery, gloves, laces, and small wares; the fourth and upper stories by A. K. Young, corset and hoop skirt maker."

The fire began in the basement of that building in the ceiling of the engine room near the elevator shaft. Spreading to the pine sheathing that lined the shaft, the fire found a ready-made chimney and spread to the rest of the building. Flames roared like a freight train while they climbed to the mansard roof. As the *Advertiser* reported it:

> The fire ran from window to window with frightening rapidity. In ten minutes flames were bursting from every opening in the roof, and ten minutes more volumes and waves of flames were rolling out from every window in the third story with such terrible force that the fate of the building was decided.

Chief Damrell heard the alarms and hurried from his home on Temple Street to reach the fire on foot. Arriving on the scene, Damrell immediately sounded the general alarm that summoned every firefighter in the city. It was 7:45 P.M., and steamer 7 was battling the blaze alone. Steamers 4 and 10 arrived moments later pulled by men who already looked exhausted. Just twenty-one minutes after the first alarm, Chief Damrell knew that the crisis was severe.

Connected to the hydrant at the corner of Kingston and Summer Streets, steamer 4 tried to hold the line in the face of searing heat, flying glass from blown out windows, and exploding fragments of granite. The men of the company risked their lives trying to extinguish a five-story inferno with hoses that spit water only to the fourth floor. As the *Boston Post* bitterly explained:

> Far up in a Mansard roof, beyond the reach of the hardest puffing engine, the fire first asserted its power. It spread along over the stout granite beneath. It leaped the street and licked up a block of Mansards on the other side. From housetop to housetop it sped compelling all beneath it to aid in the chase. . . . An acre of pine wood goes to make the Mansard roof of one of our fine modern blocks, and a fine fire it makes.

A massive block of hot granite smashed onto the sidewalk and severed the company's hose. As steamer 4 retreated, flames burst from the upper stories of the brick buildings across an alley. "The heat became so terribly intense," according to the *Advertiser,* "that it passed through the brick walls of adjoining buildings and the fronts of warehouses on the opposite sides of the streets, and communicated fire without any direct contact with flame."

By 8 P.M. the fire had jumped across Summer Street and was being met by the Boston Fire Department that was now approaching full strength. Chief Damrell knew that the battle for the building on the corner of Summer and Otis Streets would be his last chance to keep the blaze from raging totally out of control and sweeping through his city. Impervious to the danger, firemen on Otis dragged hoses up ladders while their fellow firefighters struggled up stairways to reach smoky upper stories on Summer. But as they turned on the nozzles from their hazardous perches, the brave men found almost no water pressure.

Chief Damrell made a decision. He shut down pumpers in some locations in the vain hope of getting sufficient pressure to fight the fire at others. At the end of a shut-down hose, desperate men found themselves facing the searing flames with no means of protection. "More water" was the cry. But the water never came. Within minutes the heroic battle on the corner of Summer and Otis Streets became a futile gesture.

Chief Damrell sent telegrams asking for mutual aid from cities and towns within 50 miles of Boston. The conflagration was on the loose. A battle had been lost. The chief had no intention of losing the war.

The strategy was now clear. The fire was sweeping east in a fan or half-circle shape from the block where it started. To the south the fire would eventually burn itself out on the city docks. To the north and east were the historic landmarks that stood in the heart of Boston. Whatever the effort, whatever the cost, the conflagration had to be stopped in the north and east. The broad avenues of Washington and State Streets became the last lines of defense.

As the inferno raged through Devonshire, Federal, Congress and Pearl Streets, firefighters from outlying towns rushed to Boston. The fire had progressed to districts where better water pressure finally allowed hoses to be effective. Engines were stationed on Washington Street to drench perimeter defenses while others fought on Milk, Otis, and other streets to slow the advancing flames.

Shortly after midnight, throngs of excitable men descended on the mercantile blocks that were in the path of the fire. Their interest was not curiosity, but, in the words of the *Advertiser,* "the sharp, matter-of-fact considerations of property, business, and profit."

> . . . The fire was already setting its wizard teeth upon the rear walls of the stores [when] hundreds of stalwart arms bent to the work of relieving these establishments of their most valuable contents. Every sort of vehicle that could be obtained was brought into use, and the ponderous drays were allowed to move freely all along the street, over the hose lines and among the engines, for the sake of rescuing such property as it was possible to save.

Piles of salvaged goods were simply dumped onto Boston Common where impromptu signs already announced new locations where business would be resumed. Under an amber glow that reflected in the treetops, spectators gathered to look for "relics" and watch the chaos. Some came to celebrate, almost in a party mood. As a precaution against the crowd getting out of hand, the rum shops were closed. After the gas had been shut off, shops quickly reported a shortage of candles.

Rumors also began to fly: "Chief Damrell went crazy and was taken to an asylum." The *Boston Daily Evening Transcript* advised its readers in its Monday editions that this report was false. Still, under the headline, "The Arrival of Roughs," the *Transcript* informed one and all that "the Owl train from New York which arrived here this morning was filled with a rough class of passengers," and that "many roughs have come to Boston with hopes of plunder that our citizens should remain at home tonight." Later, the *Transcript* dispelled the rumor of

New York roughs without apology, alleging instead that a "comparatively small number of such characters . . . took the train at Stamford."

Since the old post office building was sure to be consumed by fire, Gen. W. L. Burt, the postmaster of Boston, had seen to it that all mail was removed and that Faneuil Hall was readied to accept his customers on Monday morning. But historic downtown Boston and a new post office building still under construction were also in the path of the flames. By 2 A.M. Sunday, General Burt concluded that more drastic measures were needed.

After summoning the mayor and Chief Damrell to City Hall, Burt held a meeting behind closed doors. No one human being could manage such a conflagration, he insisted. To stop the spread of the flames to the north, gunpowder was needed to blow up buildings and create a fire break. He left City Hall with nine volunteers and the promise of enough powder to meet his needs.

With the assistance of General Benham, George O. Carpenter, and engineers from the nearby navy yard, General Burt secured three wagons full of explosives and went to work. Reports were that as many as fifteen buildings on Washington, Devonshire, and Water Streets were blown up to check the fire. The results of the explosions drew mixed reviews. *Harper's Weekly* considered Burt a hero, but many firemen were less enthused. The *Advertiser* was of the view that "the extraordinary expedient of blowing up buildings . . . did not apparently throw the smallest impediment in the path of the flames." By Sunday noon, Chief Damrell revoked the authority to blow up any more buildings, including several on the south side of State Street that had already been mined with powder.

The *Advertiser* described the gallant fight on Washington Street in the predawn hours of Sunday morning:

> The buildings continued from 5 to 6 A.M. to burn through and fall in, frequently endangering the lives of the brave men who were tending the engines but a few feet distant. . . . At daybreak . . . the fire was completely encircled by a line of engines. . . . The exertions of the firemen on Washington Street were heroic. . . . In spite of the difficulties here the fire was most stubbornly fought, with judgment and skill. . . . The line at Washington Street . . . was one of the most critical of all. Had the fire crossed Washington Street there is no saying where it might have been stopped. Certainly the whole territory [up to Tremont Street] would have been irrecoverably given over to the flames.

The danger to firemen and bystanders was very real. A dozen firemen lost their lives and many more were injured. The *Boston Evening Transcript* listed part of the grim toll:

> Albert C. Abbott, a member of Hose Company No. 1 of Charlestown, fell from a ladder a distance of twenty-five feet at the old post-office . . . and was severely injured about the spine.
>
> Frank Olmstead, a fireman of Steamer 1 of Cambridge . . . was injured by a wall falling from the adjoining building striking him on the head. He was taken to . . . Massachusetts General Hospital on a stretcher, where he died.

A Charlestown fireman named John Leary, had his nose severed nearly off, and his head badly cut by the breaking of glass near Jordan, Marsh & Co.'s store.

Lewis C. Thompson of Worcester, a man of about twenty-five years, was struck in the head by a falling wall on Saturday night, causing a fracture of his skull, which very soon resulted in death.

With an army of engines battling on the north and torrents of water flowing through charred streets, there was more reason for hope for success on Washington Street. The tide finally turned at the Old South Meeting House. At first, according to the *Post*, "thousands believed [the Old South] to be doomed." As streams of water played on the lower roof, a burning brand blew across the street and landed in its belfry. Roof slats on this high peak were just beginning to burn when a steamer from Portsmouth, New Hampshire, came charging up Washington Street. Having just arrived on a special train at 5:30 A.M., this steamer rushed to the scene in time to let loose a prodigious stream that soared just high enough to douse the incipient flames. The Old South was saved!

Chief Damrell's strategy was working. The eastward advance of the fire on Washington Street was stopped at the Old South, and the scope of destruction was starting to narrow. General Burt's new post office building was next in the path of the fire. Made of granite and iron with little wood, the new structure gave firemen another chance to thwart the flames. Suffering relatively minor damage, the new post office diverted the inferno and narrowed the path of the fire further.

The conflagration's final assault was now aimed directly at State Street. After a twelve-hour battle, a vigorous stand beat

Boston's Great Fire of 1872 caused sixty-five acres of total destruction. In this aerial drawing created ca. 1894, smoke is seen blanketing much of the city.
LIBRARY OF CONGRESS, PRINTS & PHOTOGRAPHS DIVISION, LC-USZ62-124128

back the fire at Devonshire and State. Just 2 blocks from Faneuil Hall, the Merchants' Exchange and post office building now became the scene of the final decisive fight.

The fire had been burning all morning from the back of the columned Merchants' Exchange building that fronted on State Street. On Sunday afternoon the sky was darkened by the smoke of the fleet of steamer engines that congregated outside. With pumpers from dozens of cities and towns throwing heavy streams of water onto roof and walls, firemen swarmed into the vast structure with tangles of hoses and knocked the fire down. Unseen inside the mammoth building, heroic fire-men had gained the upper hand. By Sunday evening Boston's crisis had passed.

The Ninth Regiment and four companies of cavalry were called out to control trainloads of spectators and bring about some order. The Dragoons, Horse Guard, and Prescott Light Guard joined the Boston Police to encircle the burned area to keep out "roughs" and the merely curious.

Boston Harbor was littered with floating beams, barrels, and boxes. On the docks piles of coal intended as winter fuel burned with a pale bluish light that would flicker over the waterfront for days.

The *Advertiser* printed the following memorable description of the ruins:

> A walk through the ruins by night reveals the desolate-ness of the scene more impressively even than one by daylight. There is a weird, grotesque beauty in the prospect that is strangely fascinating. Amidst the crumbling heaps of rubbish in the cellars there are small fires flickering sufficient to reveal the fantastic proportions of the surrounding fragments of walls, and lend a ruddy glow to the rear canopy of smoke overhanging all. . . . The mysterious, intense Rembrandt effects of fitful light and shade, the moon-light occasionally penetrating through rifts of smoke . . . the exaggerated shapes of lonely columns and irreg-ular masses of wall, the silence broken only by the occasional hoarsely given order of a fireman . . . pro-duce an impression . . .which nothing . . . can convey.

On Monday sixty-five acres of the wholesale district of
Boston was a "broad plain of ruin" without a solitary lamppost
or curbstone to fix a location. Issued military passes, "gangs of
laborers were busily at work clearing the debris. . . [or] indus-
triously digging for safes and valuables." But according to
Harper's Weekly, "familiar thoroughfares were so effectively
obliterated" that workmen and citizens "clambering over heaps
of bricks and granite blocks were utterly lost."

By the time the great conflagration was extinguished, the
flames had consumed more than 900 buildings. Estimates of
loss varied from $100 to $150 million, but the people of Boston
assumed an optimistic outlook from the very start. Unlike
Chicago, which had burned the prior year, few homes were
lost. The working people of Boston had lost warehouses and
employment, but dry goods and jobs were readily replaced.
Besides, as *Harper's* noted, there had been an oversupply of
many items before the fire. "Thus the savage roar of the flames
may in some measure be happily drowned by the peaceful,
prosperous hum of the spindles."

Before the smoke had cleared, General Burt and others
even saw the fire as the opportunity it was. The post office
would expand. New business would be developed. The narrow,
crooked streets that had been obliterated would be replaced by
broad avenues that would grace a modern Boston, its historic
landmarks still intact.

"The men who made the Old South and the Old State-
House and Faneuil Hall famous would have looked with grim
pride upon the sturdy heroism of their descendants," concluded *Harper's.* The landmarks that survived may be "in
Boston, but they are the treasures of the country."

CHAPTER 5

THE MILL RIVER FLOOD

Failure of the Williamsburg Dam

1874

The industrialists who developed the Mill River Valley knew all about the power of water. The steeper and faster the flow, the more energy that could be extracted. They knew that the steep narrow stream that dropped 700 feet from its headwaters in Williamsburg to the Connecticut River in Northampton would provide all the energy they needed for their businesses. The Mill River was a natural. Along its 7-mile length of rocky terrain, head-race canals, mill ponds, sluiceways, water wheels, and turbines were erected to harness the river's flow. Controlled and channeled, the small but mighty Mill River supplied the power for button factories, brass works, silk, cotton, and woolen mills.

In the early 1800s four villages lined the Mill River: Williamsburg, Skinnerville, and Haydenville within the town of Williamsburg, and Leeds in the town of Northampton. Five thousand people lived in the rural valley, many in white, wood-frame,

New England houses clustered in the villages along the banks of the river.

Sixty-four mills drew power from the Mill River. Businesses in the valley were not on the same scale as the great mills in Lawrence, Lowell, and Holyoke, but people in the Mill River Valley were prosperous. Owners of the local mills lived well in stately homes. Active in banks, churches, and politics, the mill owners controlled the local economy and ran local affairs. They built company housing, schools, and churches for practical reasons. A stable, moral workforce was good for the community and good for business.

Men named Hayden, Skinner, Spelman, and Dimock harnessed the power of the Mill River and made themselves powerful. Their mistake was in believing that the power of water could always be controlled.

In Massachusetts, as in the rest of New England, the problem with water-powered mills was the lack of summer rain. To solve the problem mill owners often joined together to build their own reservoir dams. After getting permission from the state legislature, mill owners constructed large earthen dams and were free to control the outflow of water however they saw fit.

The Goshen dam had controlled the headwaters of the West Branch of the Mill River since 1852. Holding spring rains for release in the dry summer months, the Goshen dam and reservoir ensured that mills in the valley would be humming and residents employed throughout the year.

By 1864 businesses in the Mill River Valley were expanding, and the mill owners felt the need for more power. Scouting the East Branch of the Mill River 3 miles above Williamsburg, Joel Hayden Sr. found the perfect site for the

Williamsburg dam. The lieutenant governor of Massachusetts, Joel Hayden Sr., owned a cotton mill and a gasworks and brass factory made of bricks, which was 600 feet long. He created Haydenville and had plenty of industrious friends. The Williamsburg Reservoir Company had no trouble securing a state charter and finding the money to build its dam.

As mill owners, Joel Hayden Sr., William Skinner, Onslow Spelman, Lewis Bodman, Lucius Dimock, William Clark, and others had plenty of experience with water and water power. They knew how to build a dam and rejected three designs supplied by contractors and engineers as too expensive. They devised their own plan for an embankment dam that cost 80 percent less than the first proposal.

Embankment dams need a solid core to keep water from filtering through the structure. Instead of a solid masonry wall or a wall of shiplap timbers, the Williamsburg Reservoir Company settled on a common New England stone wall set on bedrock or hardpan soil.

Embankment dams need a gradual slope of compacted earth piled over the core wall to keep the pressure of the water in the reservoir pushing down rather than out against the dam. Instead of a gradual slope, the Williamsburg Reservoir Company saved money. They used less fill and created a steeper slope.

At 600 feet long by 43 feet high, the Williamsburg dam flooded more than 100 acres and created a reservoir of 600 million gallons of water. But the Williamsburg dam was trouble from the start. Water oozed from the downstream base, making the ground around it swampy and wet. Vast chunks of muddy soil slid off the face of the dam after spring rain. In the first three years of the dam's life, the owners piled brush and drove timbers into the core to stabilize the structure. They added thousand of pounds of extra fill to increase the slope of the face and hauled in crushed stone to prevent erosion. They spent nearly half as much on improvements as they had spent on construction of the original dam.

Despite these efforts, Joel Hayden Sr. was quietly troubled. He knew that a faulty dam jeopardized every resident of Mill River Valley and also jeopardized the mills and homes and factories that were his whole life's work. On rainy nights in the spring, the elderly Joel Hayden would ride alone on the muddy road that led the few miles from his house to the Williamsburg dam. Unable to sleep, he would check the reservoir level, inspect the size of the leaks at the base of the dam, and reassure himself that the dam was holding. As a precaution, during stretches of bad weather, his friend and partner William Skinner moved his valuable supply of raw silk from his silk mill to high ground.

Over the years worry about the dam decreased. The reservoir company appointed a caretaker, George Cheney, who lived with his family beside the dam and kept an eye on the dam's condition. At Joel Hayden Sr.'s instructions, water levels in the reservoir were kept at a moderate level. Treated gingerly, the dam held. Except for Joel Hayden Sr., most residents of the valley forgot about the danger. Then, in November 1873 Joel Hayden Sr. died.

Joel Hayden Jr. didn't share his father's concerns about the safety of the Williamsburg dam. After his father's death, the spring rains of 1874 were allowed to fill the reservoir to its capacity, but the caretaker, George Cheney, continued to have his own doubts about the dam and its many leaks.

Dawning cool and wet, May 16, 1874, a Saturday, was just another day of work in the industrious Mill River Valley. Time was money and workers were expected to report early at the busy mills.

George Cheney was up and out of his house as usual at 6 A.M. to look over the Williamsburg dam. The reservoir was completely full, but everything looked in order. Cheney walked back to his house for breakfast with his wife, several children, and his elderly father. They were just finishing their meal at about 7:15, when a loud noise signaled the start of the disaster. "For God's sake, George, look there!" yelled Grandfather Cheney. A 40-foot-long section of the base of the dam was rapidly slipping away and washing downstream.

Running along the base of the failing dam without concern for his own safety, the caretaker opened the gate wide in the vain hope of draining the reservoir fast enough to prevent the catastrophe he had always feared. Turning back toward his house, Cheney paused to look at the face of the dam. The *Springfield Republican* recounted what he saw:

> . . . it could hardly fail in a few minutes to give way entirely; streams of water as large as a man's arm were forcing their way, new ones appearing every moment, the wall was constantly crumbling away, and its utter downfall was evidently only a question of minutes.

Telling his father to warn their neighbors, Cheney rushed to the barn, bridled his horse, and, riding bareback, bolted down the narrow road along the stream to Williamsburg. On his 3-mile dash, Cheney passed homes that would certainly be inundated in a flood, but duty told him that in this emergency he didn't have time to stop and warn each of these neighbors and friends.

Onslow Spelman saw the caretaker's horse stagger up his driveway and met Cheney outside his home. Spelman, the mill owner who supervised the Williamsburg dam, thought of his employee, Cheney, as an alarmist. When Cheney gasped out that the reservoir was going, Spelman replied that it wasn't possible. Precious minutes slipped past, as Cheney was forced to explain why he thought the dam was failing and where precisely the breach would occur.

Finally, Spelman sent Cheney to the livery stable for a fresh horse and went off to tell employees of his button factory to head for high ground. At the livery Cheney ran into the man that the media of the day would portray as their favorite hero.

Collins Graves was a lifelong resident of the Mill River Valley and was firmly rooted in his community. The son of a dairy farmer, he operated the local milk delivery business and kept his supplies in an icehouse in the basement of the Spelman mill. Cheney's word was good enough for him. "If the dam is breaking, the folks must know about it," Graves said, and with that he leaped into his milk delivery wagon and sped away, milk cans rattling, to warn hundreds of workers in the largest mills downstream in Skinnerville, Haydenville, and Leeds.

The breach of the Williamsburg dam was truly a cataclysmic event. Unlike many other failures, this was not a case where a reservoir overflowed and water washed away the top of a dam. The Williamsburg dam virtually exploded when the immense pressure of the reservoir's water blew out the base of the structure, instantaneously releasing the content of the entire reservoir. Complete devastation was assured by the steep, narrow channel of the Mill River that funneled the immense force of the water through the most populated parts of the valley.

After Cheney had spoken with Spelman, church bells began ringing a warning in Williamsburg village at about 7:45 A.M. when the flood tide hit. Onslow Spelman had just reached high ground when he heard a roar that told him that this time Cheney was right.

Witnesses described the giant wave as anywhere from 20 to 40 feet high, a wave that took fifteen to twenty minutes to pass. Like an ocean surge that strikes a shallow shore and creates a wave, the front wall of reservoir water was slightly slowed by trees, rocks, and buildings. Like a looming wave, this front wall of water grew in height and mass. Most terrifying of all, witnesses told of seeing the dark, murky form but not being able to see water. Propelled through the valley was a gigantic wall of trees, roof beams, livestock, silt, rocks, mill equipment, furniture, manufactured goods, and human beings that continued to scour much of the landscape down to bare rock.

Harper's Weekly reported the effects of the flood tide:

Trees and drift-wood obscured the waters. Spelman's button factory did not stand a moment. It rose up on the crest of the wave, and collapsed as though made of card-board. [In Williamsburg] a dozen houses lined the valley, and the inmates were forgotten in the general alarm. The waters lapped them up. Entire families were destroyed in a moment. . . . Fifty-three persons lost their lives in three minutes after Cheney's alarm was given.

As he bolted off on his mission of mercy, Collins Graves didn't see the devastating flood destroy his hometown. Shouting, "The reservoir is right here; run, 'tis all you can do!" Graves dashed downstream to warn the factory workers. "The people [in the streets] could hear it," he reasoned, "but the roar of the factories would drown any warning for the operatives."

Graves's first stop was the silk factory in Skinnerville, about a mile downstream. Wheeling into the dooryard of the mill, Graves shouted a warning to the company's bookkeeper, left in less than a minute, and began the next 1-mile leg of his race to Haydenville. Stopping first at the brass works, Graves barged into the main office to warn superintendent Charles Wentworth that the reservoir was coming, but Wentworth scoffed that it wouldn't be there for days.

Doubt crept into Graves's mind. After all, he hadn't actually seen any floodwater. Exhausted, he turned his horse back upstream, when, for the first time, he saw the horrible sight. Thinking he would lose his life, Graves whipped his horse uphill and made it to high ground with barely twenty seconds to spare. The *Springfield Daily Republican* reported:

> Here the famous ride, which will be sung in story and told to the credit of Collins Graves around the fire-sides of Williamsburg forever as the salvation of many hundred lives, ended at the hotel; the horse and rider were both exhausted, and here another herald took up the tidings.

Graves had arrived in Skinnerville about five minutes before the flood. By the time he reached Haydenville, the reservoir water was just two minutes behind him. Statistics prove

Harper's Weekly Journal of Civilization *depicted the Mill River flood as well as the
"race with the flood" made by local heroes George Cheney (on left) and
Collins Graves (on right).*

what a difference a few minutes can make. Newspapers reported only four dead in Skinnerville as workers in the silk factory were calmly evacuated minutes before the brick structure was demolished. But in Haydenville, where the floodwaters used smaller houses as battering rams to destroy a foundry and the massive brass mill, the reported toll was eighty lives. With only seconds to make an escape, many people who saw the flood coming were simply frozen from fright. The *Springfield Daily Republican* provided one such example: "Miss Carrie Bonney and Mrs. Sarah J. Ryan and child, who were among those swept away and lost, had ample time to save themselves, but were completely stupefied with terror, and, with a fixed stare, stood motionless."

In such an emergency there was no "correct" response. Some who tried to run for their lives were snatched up by the water or crushed by heavy debris. Other were swept away only to regain their senses in the arms of a stout tree. Many died in the "safety" of their own homes when the structures simply collapsed. One family was lucky to survive when apple trees in the front yard caught so much debris that they diverted the flood, preventing it from carrying their house away. An accountant learned the hard way that it was not safe to go back to the office in an effort to rescue the books. And a worker paid with his life trying to retrieve a pair of boots.

The most heroic effort, at the greatest risk of his own life, was performed by a man who received scant attention at the time. Myron Day drove a delivery or "express" wagon in the valley. When he arrived in Haydenville that Saturday morning, he heard the warnings being given in the village. Day was eager to warn his friends in Leeds, but the flood was nearly upon him. To deliver the message to the next village, he would need to race a mile downstream on a road through a narrow ravine that channeled the river and offered no escape. He knew that if he entered this race, he had to win to keep his life.

As reported by the *Springfield Daily Republican*, "lashing his horse to a foam and barely keeping ahead of the seething waves, Mr. Day, in his anxiety to save others, came near losing his own life by driving directly into the steep defile." With retreat impossible Day made it to the village of Leeds in the nick of time. Passing the Nonotuck Silk Company, Day broadcast the alarm at George Warner's button factory, while the flood was sweeping away the silk company's dam at the other end of town.

Myron Day's courage saved many lives, but seconds were precious in the village of Leeds. In spite of Day's warning, loss of life was heavy in the button factory, where twenty minutes later the flood had passed. The papers reported fifty-one lives lost. Where the button factory once stood, only a chimney remained on the scoured rock of the valley floor.

Below Leeds the slope of the valley eased as the Mill River prepared to meet the Connecticut River near the village of Florence. Spared total devastation, Florence was fated to become the dumping ground for most of the corpses and material swept away by the horrible flood. Some of the finest river-bottom agricultural land in Massachusetts was washed away and covered with debris that (if gathered together) would have covered five acres to a depth of 10 feet.

The final toll was 139 human lives lost and 146 families left destitute. As town halls and churches became impromptu morgues, help arrived from all across New England. The search for bodies lasted for days as volunteers and self-sufficient survivors attacked the maze of debris with axes, crowbars, teams of horses, and ropes.

Newspapers around the region were quick to cast blame. "Rascality, carelessness, and egotism," cried the *New York World*. "Dishonest," said the *New York Herald*. "A trap of destruction," announced the *Hartford Times*. "The builders of that dam were murderers," proclaimed the *New York Evening Mail*.

But residents of the Mill River Valley reached far different conclusions. There was plenty of blame to go around—the builders, the mill owners, the state legislature. More important to the local people was the resumption of their lives. Many of the mills were rebuilt or replaced. Mill owners rehired employees as quickly as possible, and a relief committee paid compensation up to a maximum of $300 for a family and $50 for a working man. Most people gladly accepted the money as enough for a fresh start. After all the loss of life and devastation, no lawyers went to court and no damages were paid.

Cheney, Graves, and Day received medals for their heroism and lived out their lives in the Mill River Valley. No one ever found a reason to remove what was left of the Williamsburg dam. A few miles above town, an earthen slope with a gaping hole remains hidden among the trees.

CALAMITY AT DEVIL'S BRIDGE REEF

The *City of Columbus* Tragedy
1884

On a crisp Thursday morning on Nickerson's wharf, the *City of Columbus* was preparing to leave on its regular run to Savannah. Ticket sales for the popular ship were as brisk as the January weather.

A break from the New England winter was excuse enough to board the plush steamer, but the reasons for sailing were as varied as the passenger list. Capt. S. Vance of Truro, Nova Scotia, was bound for Pensacola to take command of another ship. Brothers Herbert and George Farnsworth, ages eleven and seventeen, decided to leave their work on a farm in Townsend to start a new life in Jacksonville, Florida. Brothers Henry and Eugene McGarry bought their tickets seeking warmer weather. F. L. Hale, owner of a produce firm in Boston, was traveling on a business trip without his wife and three children. Henry Batchelder had retired from the coal business and was on his way to Florida for the rest of the winter.

One of two sister ships owned by the Boston & Savannah Steamship Company, the *City of Columbus* embarked on its scheduled run shortly after 3 P.M. on January 17, 1884, with eighty first-class passengers, twenty-two steerage passengers, and a crew of forty-five. As the 275-foot-long ship steamed out of Boston Harbor, there was plenty for its guests to admire. Described by the *Boston Evening Transcript* as a "floating palace," the steamship with its 1,500-horse-power engine sported a grand saloon over 100 feet long finished in "French walnut, mahogany, rosewood, and bird's eye maple, and upholstered in the finest crimson plush."

All was well with Capt. S. E. Wright at the helm as the ship rounded Race Point, curled beneath Cape Cod, and headed for the channel through Vineyard Sound. With more than eighteen years experience, including two years in command of the *City of Columbus,* Wright felt confident that his course was safe. The channel he chose was among the best lighted on the coast, with lighthouses at Gay Head on Martha's Vineyard, as well as at Cuttyhunk and other locations on the north and south sides of the channel.

The wind was brisk and the seas were high when the luxury vessel passed West Chop and Nobska Point near Woods Hole. But no extreme weather or natural disaster would be responsible for the loss of the *City of Columbus.* No freak occurrence, no unimagined event would lead to the ship's demise. On that dreadful night only carelessness and lack of attention caused a horrible loss of life.

"Passed Nobska, and with course west-southwest, stepped into my room to warm myself," the captain later stated. "It was very cold. Everything was working well."

Roderick McDonald was the quartermaster on the ship.

The rocky coast where the City of Columbus *wrecked is depicted in this historic engraving.* NOAA PHOTO

When the captain went below, he took over the wheel and became responsible for steering the ship down the 7-mile-wide channel. "It was a heavy blow, but clear overhead, with the horizon hazy," he remembered. "The wind was a little on our starboard bow . . . we took a southwest by west, which always took us mid-channel. The captain went below about an hour before we struck."

After the accident various officers on the ship offered varying stories on what had happened. Was the Devil's Bridge buoy to port or starboard? Was there a slight misunderstanding in the course to be steered? Were one or more officers asleep at the wrong time? Was the wind strong enough to blow the ship off course? As far as the public was concerned, the answers to these questions hardly mattered in the end. On a clear night the *City of Columbus,* while 3 miles off course, struck a well-marked reef virtually at the foot of a lighthouse that was in perfect working order. "We could see the Gay Head Lights plainly off our port bow. The light appeared closer than usual," the quartermaster admitted.

Implausibly, Captain Wright later seemed to suggest that the light was too bright: "It is so bright it sometimes confuses one; its brightness, however," he had to confess, "would not deceive one as to its bearing."

A passenger, Capt. T. L. Hammond, was another seafaring man on his way to a ship in Florida. After barely surviving the wreck, Captain Hammond offered a blunt assessment of the cause. "The officers and lookout of the *City of Columbus*, at the time of the disaster, " he believed, "were sound asleep, else they never could have allowed their vessel to go ashore on the Devil's Bridge on a bright night, and directly beneath the glare of the Gay Head light."

The *Boston Evening Transcript* sounded a similar note. "It is still a mystery why the second mate, in charge of the vessel, did not see that the ship was out of the proper course, especially when, if he was awake, he must have seen Gay Head light dead ahead."

One detail is undisputed. In the middle of the night, Captain Wright was roused from his cabin when he heard the officer of the watch say something about "port." "I jumped out of my room; thinking we had come across a vessel bound down the sound. I then cried out 'Hard a port,' not knowing but it was a vessel."

Regrettably, the watch was not reporting a vessel, but the buoy on Devil's Bridge Reef. The turn the captain ordered would have placed the vessel even further off course, but already it was too late. Almost immediately, at 3:45 A.M., the

City of Columbus tore open its keel on the deadly rocks at the southwest tip of Martha's Vineyard.

Instantly, the hull of the ship began to fill with water. In minutes the floating palace listed, then righted itself, and settled into the water at the stern. The terrifying minutes did nothing to improve the seamanship of the crew. Passengers were left to fend for themselves. Edward Leary was the lookout. After the crash there was great confusion; Leary confirmed that it was every man for himself.

The *Boston Post* observed that "the *Columbus* was manned by an inexperienced and undisciplined crew, which, in case of emergency, were no more to be depended upon for service than so many school boys."

As passengers rushed up to the deck, few wore life preservers. Most were simply washed off the ship as quickly as they climbed the stairs—victims of massive waves that continued to swamp the vessel.

The crew focused its attention on trying to launch the lifeboats. "Launched port No. 6 boat, which was immediately capsized," reported the captain. "All of the boats were cleared away but were immediately swamped," he later told reporters.

The quartermaster told a different story:

> Got a knife to cut away the lashings of the boats, and went to No. 2 lifeboat. . . . The ship had just begun to cant when we got the lee lashings cut. The vessel careened over, and we had to abandon the attempt to get the lifeboat free. Some were at work on the port side boats, which were plunged under the water, all but one, by the tipping of the vessel on that side. I slid down a rope to the one boat that was afloat on the port

side. . . . I jumped for her, and fell overboard. The next sea that swung her toward the vessel enabled me to catch hold of the gunwale. . . . Then the boat suddenly filled under a heavy sea. Three of the men on board jumped into the water, thinking she would sink, and they were drowned before they could reach the ship.

Captain Vance, the passenger headed for Pensacola, told of a similar ordeal after being washed off the deck of the steamer:

I caught hold of the boat which had been put over and stove alongside. . . . I got into her and looked for my knife to cut her adrift, but could not find it. I was in the boat four or five minutes when she capsized with me under her. I let go and swam from the wreck. After clearing the wreck, I turned on my back and floated, not trying to swim. I looked up and saw a swamped boat drifting toward me. She was about forty feet away, and no one was in her. I swam to her and got in. Was capsized twice . . . it was a fearful struggle, but it was for my life.

Within thirty minutes of the crash, most of the passengers were dead. Eugene McGarry was one of the lucky ones who were able to climb into the ship's rigging.

The waves came tumbling over the deck, sweeping away one person after another, and when one of [the lifeboats] was almost ready to launch it was turned over and a number of women sank from sight. For a while I stayed on the forward deck, near the pilot house, which seemed to be the safest place; but after some time had passed all who had gathered there found they must climb aloft. The sea broke over the vessel and we saw the cabin and pilot house swept away.

For the fifty or so souls who now clung to ropes and stays in the rigging, a grueling test began. The clear-cut rules were unforgiving. Hold tight with your grip or die! Eugene McGarry again remembered what he had seen: "One poor fellow clung to the rail, and resisted one wave after another. It seemed to me he was there half an hour making a desperate fight for his life. He could not move to a better place, and was finally lost."

Passenger Tibbetts saw a young man take a deck of cards out of his pocket and throw them into the sea, not wanting to appear before God with a pack of cards in his pocket. Tibbetts's roommate in a first-class cabin was an engineer from Roxbury, whom he saw "drop out of the rigging, frozen to death," while the crew carried on indifferently, passing the time, waiting to be rescued.

The *Boston Evening Transcript* described the death of a crewman and one passenger as follows:

John Roach, a coal-heaver, dangled from the mainstay for two hours with his hands and legs about the mainstay. At length his struggles grew feebler until he dropped into the sea. A passenger was astride the stay and clung there from 5 until 10 A.M. when he relinquished the fight for life and fell into the ocean.

After the disaster Horatio Pease, keeper of the Gay Head light, expressed surprise that no flares or distress signals were sent up by the steamer. The omission meant that a lifesaving crew was delayed for several hours. "Just before dawn I sent my assistant to summon the people living on the headland. He went as fast as possible from house to house, but it was slow work. The whole town of about 150, all told, was finally aroused and came flocking to the shore."

Horatio Pease found an ample supply of eager volunteers who risked their lives by manning a lifeboat and rowing into wind and wave for thirty minutes to span the three-quarters of a mile out to the wreck. All of the men in the lifeboat crew were what the papers called "natives of Gay Head." More accurately, they were part of the Native-American community living at Gay Head. Purser Spaulding stated:

> The life boat crew of the Massachusetts Humane Society were the bravest men I ever saw. They are all volunteers, but they came out in the terrible sea and rescued us, risking their own lives a thousand times. These men saved that morning 20 lives.

The first lifeboat arrived on the scene at about 10 A.M., but could only approach to within 50 yards for fear of capsize caused by the ship's debris. Seven men who clung to the shrouds were persuaded to jump into the sea and were pulled into the rescue boat. Exhausted, the lifeboat crew rowed the survivors back to shore where a second crew was recruited to return to the wreck. By the time the second Gay Head crew reached the wreck, it was afternoon and the revenue cutter *Dexter* had arrived on the scene. Thirteen more frigid survivors splashed into the sea and were delivered to the cutter by the Gay Head crew.

Still, twenty more bodies clung to the frigid rigging of the sunken steamer. It was impossible to say who was dead and who was still alive. Nonetheless, the time had arrived for the most widely recognized hero of the day, Lt. John Underhill Rhodes.

Commanding a small boat from the *Dexter*, Rhodes inched close to the wreck just as the Gay Head lifeboats had done. George and Herbert Farnsworth, the young farm workers from Townsend, were, according to the *Boston Evening Transcript*, "perfectly willing to plunge into the sea when so ordered by the crew of the relief boat though their arms and legs were so stiff and their hands so numb that it was almost impossible to move them at first." The boys were carried to safety by the first relief boat Rhodes commanded.

Brothers Henry and Eugene McGarry also jumped into the sea. Eugene lived to tell the tale. "I had taken off my coat and shoes, and waited until my brother made the attempt before I tried. He sank, but when I jumped a big billow carried me a long distance, and one of the boat-men caught me with a boathook." According to the *Boston Post*, "Lt. Rhodes jumped for Eugene McGarry [really Henry], but the boat was lifted 15 feet on a crest. . . . The poor man was not seen afterwards."

When Captain Wright fell into the sea, the rescue boat ferried him back to the cutter. Now, only two human forms still clung to the rigging. Lieutenant Rhodes was determined to save them, even at the peril of his own life.

After rowing back to the wreck with another sailor, Rhodes tied a rope to his waist and jumped into the frigid water. But his first attempt failed when a piece of wreckage struck him in the leg. He was pulled aboard the relief boat and taken back to the cutter.

He had suffered only a cut. He changed into dry clothing and realized that it was now almost 4 P.M. Darkness was coming fast. The lieutenant continued his efforts to retrieve those two men. Once more back to the wreck, Rhodes swam to the lee rigging and climbed into the steamer's shrouds. The first body was lifeless and firmly held by ropes. He cut the ratlines and let the body fall into the water. The last body remaining in the rigging was found in the same condition. Again, Rhodes cut the body down and hauled the last two victims of the horrible wreck back to the mother ship.

Including passengers and crew, the wreck of the *City of Columbus* took one hundred lives. In the words of the *Nantucket Journal*, "The hardships to which the sufferers had been exposed will be realized when it is stated that after their rescue four of them died on board the cutter, and that not a woman or child was saved."

Captain Wright was relieved of his license. He had commanded his last ship.

SUBURBAN NIGHTMARE

The Collapse of Bussey Bridge

1887

Commuting to work from the suburbs did not begin with the automobile in the twentieth century. By 1887 thousands of workers already made the daily trek into Boston by rail. The Boston & Providence Railroad and other lines scheduled frequent commuter service from suburbs like Dedham to the business heart of the city.

Much as they do today, white-collar executives, office workers, and salesclerks left home with a bag lunch and a morning paper to begin the daily grind. After meeting friends at the station, they would board the 7 A.M. train without a second thought for the routine journey downtown.

Commuting by rail was safe. Since the creation of the Board of Railroad Commissioners eighteen years earlier, the Boston and Providence Railroad had not had an accident that resulted in the loss of life or even serious injury. But, during the morning commute on the Dedham Branch on March 14, 1887, the reputation of the railroad instantly changed.

As usual on a Monday morning, conductor William H. Alden "made up the train" at Dedham by ordering the brakeman to have nine cars. With eight years of experience on the Dedham Branch, conductor Alden knew that extra capacity would be needed on a busy commuting day. Behind the steam locomotive, Alden provided for eight passenger coaches and a final "combination" or smoker car—really a baggage car that admitted gentlemen passengers who wanted to smoke.

After leaving Dedham at 7 A.M., the train reached Roslindale, where it took on a heavy load of passengers—what railroad men called "human freight." Without realizing the importance of their decisions, 200 to 300 commuters selected their seats on that fateful Monday morning.

Mary F. Young discovered a crowd of people on the platform. "My friends and I walked along, trying to find the least-occupied car. We thought first that we would take one of the last cars, but we changed our minds and took one of the last seats in the third car from the engine." Their selection may have saved their lives.

Sadie Dowe was used to sitting in a car in the middle of the train. "Almost every day I take the fourth or fifth car in the train at Roslindale because I meet in it friends from Jamaica Plain, but fortunately today I was compelled by their crowded condition to go forward into the third car." Her reluctant choice would allow her to escape with only an injured hip.

The train pulled out of Roslindale station at 7:18 A.M. with engineer Walter E. White at the controls of the steam engine "Torrey," weighing over thirty-two gross tons. Engineer White, a fifty-two-year-old veteran, had spent virtually his entire adult life on the Boston & Providence Railroad. After thirty-one years as an engineer on the Dedham branch, the physical appearance of the tall, robust man suited his occupation. As described by the *Boston Globe,* the engineer's hair grew sparsely on the crown of his head, but it was "thick and luxuriant in the 'mutton chops'" adorning the face.

The journey from Roslindale to the next stop at the Forest Hills station was a little over a mile and usually lasted about four minutes. About halfway between the two stations, trains passed over Bussey Bridge, which carried the tracks at an angle across South Street not far from the Arnold Arboretum. About forty feet above street level, the bridge spanned 150 feet between two old stone abutments that were set into high embankments that extended beyond the bridge at both ends and were themselves coated with stone.

The Bussey Bridge boasted a remarkable history. Originally built entirely of wood, many parts were covered with tin in its early days to prevent fires caused by belching locomotives. In 1870 the wooden truss on the west side of what some people called the "Tin Bridge" was replaced by rectangular iron, known as a Parker truss. In 1876 the railroad hired Edmund Hewins, representing the Metropolitan Bridge Company, to move the Parker truss from the west to the east side of the bridge and to build a new iron truss (a Hewins truss) on the west side.

In hindsight several things went wrong when the bridge was reconstructed in 1876. For starters the Metropolitan Bridge Company never existed. It was a figment of the inexperienced Hewins's imagination. More significantly, tracks were attached to the bridge by hangers that were merely welded straps rather than forged iron. The hangers were off-center, cracked, and invisible to inspection. Designed to carry two tracks, only one track crossed the Bussey Bridge—on the west side. As later investigation discovered, at a time when trains were getting longer and locomotives heavier, the Hewins truss and defective hangers carried 80 percent of the weight of the trains that passed over the bridge.

Running about five to seven minutes late, engineer White reached the Bussey Bridge with his train traveling at (in his estimation) 12 to 15 miles per hour. Others thought the speed may have been as fast as 30 miles per hour on the downhill grade past Roslindale.

White recalled that everything was all right when the train entered the Dedham (south) end of the bridge. The engineer felt no swaying or settling. The crossing was routine. But at the Boston (north) end, a sudden jerk grabbed White's attention as the front of his engine lifted slightly. As the "drivers" or massive drive wheels at the rear of the engine reached the edge of the span, White felt a sudden shock and spun around to see what the problem was.

The problem, White knew in an instant, was a horrible disaster. As he recounted to the *Evening Transcript:*

> I looked around and the forward car went off the track and the coupling broke. [About four or five car lengths past the bridge,] "I reversed the engine and was about to stop, when I looked back and saw the first and second cars off the track . . . and saw a cloud of smoke rise, and then I knew they had gone through the bridge.
>
> The train stopped before I did, so that it didn't strike me after it broke away; . . . it flashed across me that help more than we could give was needed, and so I threw the running-gear forward and went for Forest Hills as fast as I could, blowing the whistle and both

the fireman and I waving our hands toward the wreck to let people know that something had happened; [I] told the station agent to telegraph for doctors and ambulances. [After about three minutes] I backed up to the bridge again and started in to help, but couldn't do much, for my strength and courage were all gone.

In the fleeting moment before the engineer turned to see a cloud of dust where the bridge had been, mayhem had occurred. When the hangers snapped as the drive wheels of the engine passed over them, the track and ties were left unsupported. But the strength of the rails allowed the track to sag for a heartbeat or two before the entire structure twisted and cracked and smashed onto the street below. That brief pause, though, saved the lives of the passengers in the first three cars behind the locomotive.

In the first seconds of Bussey Bridge's fatal fall, the slow sag of the rails made the first car rise up when it reached the abutment on the Boston end, jumping its front wheels off the track and tearing away its rear "truck" or back wheels. As the sag increased, the second car clipped the abutment with a hard jolt but was pushed beyond the bridge when the rest of the train smashed into it and crumbled its back end.

Passengers in car three may have been the luckiest. Their coach collided with the second car so hard that the wreckage of the two cars locked together. As all of its wheels were torn off, its floor nearly demolished, and both sidewalls shattered, the third car was pulled over the abutment to safety by the second car.

Of the twenty-three people who died, most were in car four and were killed instantly. The bottom half of the car struck square into one of the bridge's stone abutments with such force that the roof tore loose and landed on the tracks beyond the bridge. After striking the abutment, the rest of the shattered carriage of car four dropped in pieces 40 feet to the street below. As the *Boston Post* explained it, "The body of the car was literally ground to pieces against the abutment, and the bits of wood, iron, upholstery, and human beings were strewn on the road beneath."

The two impacts with the abutment and street would have been devastating enough, but passengers in unlucky car four were pummeled even more. The front of the fifth car smashed into the remains of car four and telescoped to nearly half its length. Car six fell on its side diagonally across the street on top of car four and amazingly beneath what was left of car five.

Like lemmings, cars seven and eight followed their leaders to smash into the wreckage below. Car seven somehow protected its passengers by landing upright in the street—comparatively unscathed. Car eight fell heavily onto its side and its walls were badly shattered.

The wildest ride was reserved for the gentlemen smokers in the baggage car, which did a flip on its way down and landed on its roof. A Mr. Pike of Roslindale provided a full description of his ordeal:

> Just as we reached the bridge, I felt a . . . tremor, which swayed the car . . . from side to side. . . . All at once I was aware that the car . . . was tipping over to the left, actually going over into that great deep hole below. . . . I had presence of mind enough to catch hold of the wooden cleats which are nailed to the studding of the baggage car, and then over we went. Baggage rolling

and skipping around the car, men jumping and holding on . . . others making for the door, and still others rolling and jumping around as best they could to keep away from the trunks and boxes that were everywhere at once. . . . [The impact] jarred me terribly, but I managed to keep my grip and still held my balance until the car ceased to crash and sway.

Several survivors were able to tell harrowing tales of their escape. Mr. W. E. Whittemore of Boston suffered a swollen eye and bruised face but managed to survive in the obliterated fourth car. "The first sensation was that of suffocation, and it appeared to me that the sides of the car were coming together, while the top of the car was sinking. . . . I found myself on my right side with my hand pinioned between the side of the car and the stone-work on which the end of the bridge had rested."

According to the *Boston Globe*, John Murphy was also in the fourth car accompanied by his daughter.

I felt the bridge sinking under me. We grabbed hold of the seats, and in an instant all the people and the seats of the car came tumbling down on us. I had one leg pinned down under me. . . . My body was under a pile of seats, and directly in front of me was a young man who appeared to be dead. At first none of us could move.

Murphy's daughter was badly crushed, and according to the *Boston Post*, was not expected to live.

As the dust began to clear, one survivor surveyed the terrible sight of the wrecked train, "everything being piled up in such confusion, the bleeding and crushed bodies of the unfortunate passengers seeming to be mixed up promiscuously with the broken-up cars, so that it seemed that nearly all had been killed." Another passenger remembered injured fellow passengers pouring out of the wrecked train.

P. W. A. Pickard of engine 18 Roslindale was one of the first firemen to reach the wreck. He recalled a scene that resembled a giant kindling-wood factory blown to pieces. Several witnesses noted that the entire span of the bridge was gone—the iron trestle work all mixed up with the wreck of the cars and one iron rail rising above the ruins bent like an oxbow. For many it was remarkably quiet, except for the moans of the wounded and dying.

Engineer White's intuitive decision to speed to the next station for help proved to be a fortunate choice. Firefighters with engine 18 promptly responded to douse a small fire that started in the wreckage near one of the small coal heating stoves that were standard in each car. A special train carrying doctors from Park Square in downtown Boston rushed to the scene so that doctors might treat the wounded and dying. For the most part, though, rescue and aid were afforded by local citizens who responded to the call.

In all manner of horse-drawn buggies, wagons, and carts, laborers and workmen who moments before had been going about their business dropped what they were doing to help in the rescue effort. Because many of the dead and injured passengers lived within a mile of the wreck, residents knew that they were coming to the aid of neighbors, relatives, and friends.

With crowbars, axes, saws, and jackscrews, the community set to work. Ted Koppman, who owned a shoe store in

Roslindale, arrived in his stocking feet, discovered Ed Norris injured in the road, placed him in his cart, and cared for him at his store.

J. H. Lennon, a fish dealer from Forest Hills, thought that he was the first man on the scene with an axe: "I went to one car from which I heard cries and moans. Here I found several passengers pinned in the debris. One poor woman was pinned down by a seat, with the body of a man across her." Later, Lennon was distressed to discover that a man was alive at the bottom of a pile of three dead bodies. Although his rescuers worked as quickly as possible, the man died soon after being extricated from the wreckage.

According to the *Boston Post:*

> One of the first bodies reached was that of a woman who was pinned down in the car, with the face jammed down between two sills, and in a most shocking condition. That she was alive seemed doubtful; still, the body was moved, when, to the terror of her rescuers, it was found that the head and one arm were severed from the body as though done by a knife.

Sadie Dow remembered only that she had just paid her fare, heard a terrible crash, and was thrown across the car onto the arm of another seat. She came to on the side of the road where two gentlemen named Reed and Weeks had placed her after pulling her out a window.

All of the dead and injured were removed from the massive wreck in under forty minutes. In fact the local rescue and recovery effort was so speedy and efficient that the final tally of injured could not be accurately made. Estimates placed the number at 150, but many injured passengers simply walked home and weren't counted. Others were carried off in wagons to shops or the homes of neighbors. Some of the most seriously injured were carried to a local fire station rather than to Massachusetts General or Boston City Hospital. Doctors feared that the victims would not survive a longer trip.

In keeping with efficiencies that would be unheard of today, the official inquiry into the tragic collapse of Bussey Bridge began on March 15, 1887—the day after the accident. After holding thirteen days of hearings, the railroad commissioners reported their findings to the state legislature within a month. Faulty work by Hewins and lax oversight by the railroad received most of the blame.

On the same day the hearings began, a crew of one hundred men set to work to clean up the wreck. Wielding axes and crowbars and aided by a block and tackle hoisted by a locomotive on the track above, the scene was cleared within forty-eight hours as twenty policemen kept crowds at bay. The Boston & Providence Railroad estimated that it would take only two additional days to replace the fallen structure with a temporary wooden bridge.

CHAPTER 8

THE BENCHMARK WINTER STORM

Trapped by a Blizzard
1888

Generations of New Englanders had seen their share of winter weather before March 11, 1888. Folks in the Northeast were used to heavy snow and cold winters. A frigid blast in early March was—and is—to be expected in this part of the world.

When snow started to fall on that raw Sunday night in 1888, only children hoping to skip school felt any reason to be excited. Even as ten inches or more of white stuff piled up by Monday morning, the *Worcester Evening Gazette* saw fit to label the storm as only "storm No. 23." Most folks regarded the March snow with a jaunty good humor. While reporting that it was not violent but a storm that was moist and sticky, the writer for the *Gazette* gazed out the window and noted with tongue in cheek that the probabilities were that the storm "will no doubt keep on until it stops." The *Gazette* didn't know how right it was!

During the winter of 1888, Massachusetts had experienced colder than average temperatures but relatively little snow. The storm that was about to change all that began with a cold low-pressure front that moved east from the Rocky Mountains and passed through the Midwest. At the same time another low full of moisture from the Gulf of Mexico began to surge out of Georgia and head up the East Coast.

A classic nor'easter, so familiar to folks in New England, was brewing. But the storm that arrived on March 11, 1888, held a surprise that made it different. Spinning in the waters of Long Island Sound, the wet southern storm grew to near hurricane force—and then stalled in place for forty-eight hours. From Sunday night until Wednesday morning, the Long Island low hurled heavy precipitation west toward New England, while the sharp western cold front draped a wall of frigid air across the region. Gale force winds buffeted Cape Cod and the islands. While Boston hovered around the freezing mark, western Massachusetts shivered with temperatures in the teens.

For Massachusetts, from Worcester west, this was a formula for disaster. While only 12 inches of slushy snow fell in Boston, 32 inches were reported in Worcester and 36 inches in Pittsfield. Driven by high winds, moist, sticky snow drifted to the height of rooftops and clogged pathways like cement. The combination of deep, heavy snow; bitter cold; and relentless gale force winds made the blizzard of '88 unique.

Before the advent of satellites and weather radar, weather reports were pieced together from local observations collected over telegraph lines. By midday on Monday, March 12, 1888, the weight of the soggy snow was snapping telegraph wires and pulling down poles like dominoes. Communication was cut off. Most people in Massachusetts were left with no way to forecast the track of the storm. In effect they were blind to what was coming.

"Boston Isolated by the Blizzard" declared the headline in the *Boston Daily Globe,* reporting the loss of rail and telegraph lines to Hartford, New York, and points south. After "blinding snowfall and a high wind, which at 2 P.M. reached nearly 50 miles per hour," the *Globe* wrongly predicted that Tuesday would be cold and clearing.

In Springfield, the *Springfield Union* reported that the city was "practically cut off from the outside world. No trains could run north, south, or west. . . . The means of communication by telegraph were not much better. The wires are down south and east and the linemen cannot reach the breaks on account of the railroad blockade."

By Monday afternoon cities in western Massachusetts began to feel the effects of what they still considered a typical large storm. While trains were delayed and telegraph lines were falling, residents reverted to tried-and-true measures to cope with the lousy weather. The *Worcester Evening Gazette* still described Monday as a "bleak and beautifully flowing day" and carried the news that "evening hackmen early shifted from wheels to runners" and that "relief parties were sent out by parents to meet children or young women coming from work."

Toward Monday evening cars on horse-drawn street railways in Worcester, Springfield, and Northampton were abandoned in drifts as drivers and horses struggled back to their stations. With the closing of the street railways, the *Springfield Union* also reported the use of sleighs with runners as rescue vehicles. "Women and girls were picked up on the streets by persons having sleighs, some of them being almost overcome."

Still, the general mood reported by the local press was lighthearted. As businesses closed early and transportation failed, working people and travelers quickly looked for accommodations. As the *Worcester Evening Gazette* observed, "The hotels were full of storm bound people last evening. Some took it good naturedly, and some did not. Both kinds stayed just the same."

Before the invention of tin cans, beer was a perishable commodity. As a result, during the siege, stranded travelers consumed beer first, followed later by supplies of hard liquor. Sporting a billiards and pool room, Cooley's Hotel in Springfield was a lively location at which to weather a winter storm. After forming a committee to secure entertainment for Monday evening, the *Springfield Union* reported that the "commercial travelers" were able to hire Murray and Murphy of "Our Irish Visitors" for a pleasant entertainment. The paper further explained that "the inmates of the hotel have made arrangements for a musical entertainment for themselves [Tuesday] evening." After their ordeal the "inmates" with walrus mustaches and derby hats proudly posed for a photograph in front of the hotel when the snow subsided.

By Tuesday morning, though, the blizzard continued unabated, and the realization grew that this was no ordinary storm. "It is said that even joy may become a burden," pondered the *Springfield Union,* "and it is certain that the element of exiled enjoyment that was so prominent during the first day and night of the great storm . . . and imparted to it so much of the spirit of a jolly 'lark' has altogether departed. The crowds of women and girls cut off from their homes and bestowed in hotels and other quarters began to grow homesick."

People began to worry. The storm had become a calamity according to Tuesday's *Springfield Union,* and the "scene presented on the streets . . . was grotesque in the highest degree." The village of Ware faced a "milk famine." In the Berkshire

Frank Leslie's Illustrated Newspaper *came out the week of March 24, 1888 with a black "BLIZZARD" banner and this dramatic illustration depicting New Yorkers being blown over by the wind.*

Hills homes and factories were running dangerously low on heating coal. Holyoke was buried, and the roof of a mill was collapsed by snow. "Every street [was] blockaded to travel by drifts varying from four to fifteen and even twenty feet."

In Hadley the *Northampton Daily Herald* reported snow "anywhere from 4 feet to 25 feet deep" with "teams of men . . . busily engaged in digging through the drifts." Strong winds blew mountains of snow in swirling confusion. One street might be blown clear of snow while around the corner drifts reached above first-story windows. In Northampton shopkeepers dug tunnels through the drifts, extending from their front doors to the middle of the street.

Folks who lived in rural areas generally fared well during the blizzard. Self-reliant to some degree, rural families were used to isolation and fending for themselves in a harsh winter. The impact on urban dwellers was much different. This blizzard was the first monster storm to hit New England after the construction of railroad and telegraph lines. The blizzard proved just how vulnerable those early transportation and communication facilities were and just how much urban dwellers depended on them.

In New England stories of stranded trains and passengers dominated newspaper coverage of the storm. The compelling human drama of being stranded away from home was frought with real danger and reminded one and all that such a fate could befall anyone.

Throughout western Massachusetts, freight trains, long-distance passenger trains, and local "accommodation" trains were all unexpectedly trapped between stations. While tracks were clear on windblown open plains, dense wet snow had packed onto tracks where railroad lines ran near embankments or through cuts in hilly terrain. In quick order stalled trains were smothered by more snow. The *Springfield Union* described the scene when rescuers approached a stalled freight: "When the freight train was reached the first thing seen was the tip of the engine's smoke stack and the snow was piled about it as if by the use of shovels and tamping it had been put there. Every crevice was filled and the cars which were open were packed full of snow and it was wedged between and under them so that all the power in the combined engines of the road could not have moved them."

As one stalled freight train blocked the road, a passenger express became trapped behind it 7 miles from the safety of Springfield. Near Amherst a locomotive jumped the track in a collision with hard-packed snow. Plows mounted on the front of engines simply broke on impact with the monstrous drifts. The usual snow removal tactics were just not working.

Armies of men were recruited to dig the trains out with shovels. Typical pay was $1.07 per day. Again, the *Springfield Union* told readers what was required:

> The bank [around the engine] was fully 18 feet high. The only way to work was to set the men shoveling in tiers. It was truly discouraging work, and at half past 2 [A.M.], with one locomotive in the drift and the other two unable to move, it was decided to give up.

A businessman named McGregor, a passenger on the stalled express train, described snowbound life:

> The train became stuck in the drifts at about 2:20 Monday afternoon, and at first most of the 165 passengers

seemed to regard it as a good joke. There was a big raid on the dining car when night came, but there was enough food for all, for the one meal, at least, and everybody was happy. That evening there was a concert on the train and festivities of one kind or another were kept up till a late hour.

When an emergency befell a passenger train, the conductor was responsible for the well-being of all onboard. During the blizzard of '88, it was a responsibility that conductors took seriously. As the stranded passengers began to face their second day in the frigid drifts, the mood inevitably turned glum. Provisions were nearly gone. Food and fuel for heat were both running low.

To live up to their obligations, conductors slogged through snow to a nearby farmhouse, struggled to the next station, or found ways to lead their passengers to safety. On one train the conductor sheparded about half his customers onto a rescue train and then to a safe hotel before the heavy drifts stalled even the rescue engines.

More typically, conductors found their way to a nearby rural home where a farm family opened their larders to save strangers in the storm. The Moran family lived close to the stranded express outside Springfield and took many of the passengers into their home for breakfast on Tuesday morning. The conductor of the drawing room car carried food back to the train to feed the rest, food that, according to the *Springfield Union*, "Mrs. Moran and her daughter willingly stayed up all night to cook."

The efforts of the conductors were often a true ordeal. Conductor F. A. Wise set out on foot to reach the nearest sta-

tion only a third of a mile away. To avoid getting lost in the blizzard, he followed a barbed wire fence that tore his clothes. The
Northampton Daily Herald continued his story:

> For six hours he battled with the elements and was sev-
> eral times about ready to give up. In some cases he
> plunged into drifts up to his shoulders, and then he
> went methodically to work. First, he patted the snow
> down in front of him with his hands, then he bent for-
> ward and pressed it down further until he could extri-
> cate his feet and trample it down. . . . All the time he
> had to contend with the furious storm, so blinding that
> he only knew he was on the right way by feeling for the
> fence. Some idea of what he suffered can be gained
> from the fact it took him more than three-quarters of
> an hour to reach the depot after he left the fence—a
> distance of less than 70 feet.

By Wednesday afternoon the storm began to let up. Men
with shovels and rescue trains were able to make progress. Still
desperate measures were needed. On the railroad lines the
usual plows were ineffective, so locomotives were employed as
battering rams. The *Northampton Daily Herald* told how rescuers used four locomotives. Three were hitched together "and
the fourth was used to pull the others out of the snow if they
should get stuck." The story elaborated on the crude but effective plowing technique:

> Having gone as far as they are able to, the engines pull
> back for about 300 feet and plunge into the drift again.
> . . . the only safe and reliable thing to do is to drive the

strong and resolute engine into the snow "head fore-most." Some 30 men are employed with the engines in shoveling.

By Wednesday evening passengers had been freed from stalled trains, passages had been cleared down the center of city streets, and the hotels had begun to empty. Coal, milk, and meat supplies were starting to get through. Life was beginning to return to normal.

Some deaths resulted from the storm. A young student at a school in Hadley tried to ride his horse home at the height of the blizzard and froze to death in a deep drift about a mile from his village. Joseph Dunkin, a railroad employee, died in a freak accident when a lever on a plow blade swung loose at high speed and struck him under the chin.

Thomas Kennedy, blinded by snow, wandered into a swamp on his way home from work at a local mill. He was lucky to survive the night with only frostbitten feet. A milkman found him and shoveled him out of a drift in the morning.

For all the fury and hardship, though, Massachusetts and the rest of New England seemed to come through the history-making blizzard with pluck to spare. Still, there were lessons to be learned. The blizzard of '88 demonstrated the value of subway transportation and underground utility lines. After the storm the use of horse-car lines and telephone poles in city streets rapidly came to an end.

CHAPTER 9

BIRTH OF THE DEADLIEST KILLER

The Spanish Influenza
1918

Late in the summer of 1918, Massachusetts, like the rest of the country, was hard in the grip of war. Day after day, bold headlines in every newspaper blared the news of the latest developments on the battlefields of Europe. Citizens eagerly devoured information about the ebb and flow of the armies that were fighting a war in which Allied victory was still far from certain. Most people had friends, relatives, or neighbors who were fighting for their country. Readers reacted to reports of an infantry surge at St. Quentin or a cavalry charge in Macedonia with an immediate sense of hope or fear or dread.

The public was in no mood for subtle distinctions. Germans were despicable "Huns." You either supported the war effort or you were a traitor. National laws encouraged the public mood. Criticizing the government could land you in jail. The post office could refuse to deliver printed material that did not enthusiastically support the war.

Under these wartime conditions, newspapers in Massachusetts responded like most newspapers throughout the country. Gruesome reports from the front lines in Europe would often include the most positive spin possible. Huns and their sympathizers were vilified. Bad news was avoided if at all possible. Better to boost the spirits of citizens on the home front—or divert their attention with the exploits of the Boston Red Sox as they pummeled the hapless Cubs to win the World Series.

Newspaper editors wanted to do their part to keep up morale for the war effort. What were they supposed to do when a vicious epidemic began killing thousands of people in their own hometowns?

Commonwealth Pier was the site of what the navy called a "receiving ship"—really a ramshackle barracks for thousands of sailors passing through Boston on their way to war. Arriving from scattered ports from around the country and around the world, sailors were crowded together in drafty quarters before moving on to their next assignments. Illness and disease was all too common. A few extra seamen coming down with the "grippe" in late August was not an event that was worthy of mention in the Boston papers.

But sixty hospital tents on a Brookline hilltop were hard to ignore. On September 10 the *Boston Evening Transcript* carried an article on page 4 that reported 1,109 sailors sick with the "old-fashioned grippe," including 10 percent of the 5,000 men quartered at Commonwealth Pier. A photograph of the tented hospital included a caption assuring readers that the victims had been isolated. Besides, the paper reported, "the cases in Boston are mild."

The rest of the Boston papers ignored the spreading disease. On September 12, a story on page 12 of the *Boston Globe* noted the quarantine of a brigade at Camp Devens in Ayer

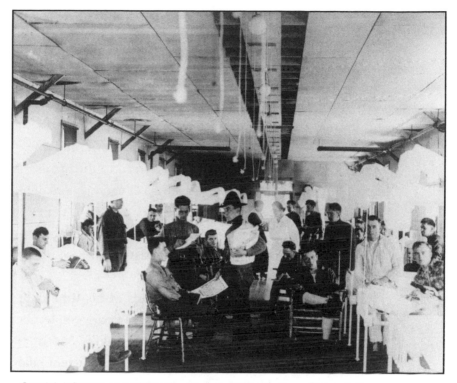

Spanish influenza spread from Commonwealth Pier to Camp Devens in Ayers, Massachusetts, killing 787 soldiers.
LIBRARY OF CONGRESS, PRINTS AND PHOTOGRAPHS DIVISION, LC-USZ62-108266

attributed to cases of measles. On the next day, though, page 4 of the same paper announced that seven doctors and eleven nurses were stricken with the grippe at the Chelsea Naval Hospital, that one nurse had died from complications of pneumonia, and that the illness had spread to Camp Devens.

Still, local reports continued to cast the news in a positive light. Rarely referred to as Spanish influenza, stories advised staying out of crowds as the best way to avoid becoming ill. If you caught the "grippe," bed rest and aspirin were touted as reliable cures.

Rear Adm. Spencer S. Wood made his views clear. The illness was "plain grippe without any fancy names." Besides, it
was "unfair to the navy to have the public believe that sailors
brought the disease and spread it hereabouts."

Admiral Wood was confident and had some logic on his
side, but he was also completely wrong. Early in 1918 the
Spanish influenza, which may have been born in Kansas,
infected a giant army base, and soon spread to the armies in
Europe. The first wave of the disease was dangerous and debil-
itating, but similar to the common strain of the influenza or
grippe that the world was familiar with. Deaths rates increased
when the flu led to pneumonia, but the vast majority of victims
survived. Soldiers knew it as the "three-day fever."

What Admiral Wood and most doctors of his time didn't
know was that viruses mutate and change. In early September
of 1918, no one knew that the Spanish influenza had transformed itself from a routine grippe to a virulent, efficient killer.
Simultaneously, from the Commonwealth Pier in Boston,
from Brest in Europe, and from Sierra Leone in Africa, a
deadly second wave of Spanish influenza exploded across the
globe to snuff out twenty-five million lives.

Symptoms of influenza usually include fever, chills, body
aches, headaches, stuffiness, coughing, and nausea. The
Spanish influenza included all of these symptoms to an
intense degree as well as a few others that caused terror in
the population. Coughing might be continuous and so severe
as to tear muscle from bone. Earaches, intense joint pain,
delirium, and exhaustion were common. Many victims
would bleed profusely from the nose, eyes, or ears, or choke
on bloody foam that bubbled up from pneumonia-clogged
lungs.

Although some people thought that Massachusetts was suffering from bubonic plague or black death, the Spanish influenza became known as the purple plague. Severe pneumonia prevents oxygen from entering the blood and causes "cyanosis" that turns the skin deep purple or blue. The huckleberry color was common in the 1918 epidemic, and it was an almost certain sign that the victim was fatally ill.

The horrifying symptoms spread terror among the citizens of Massachusetts, in spite of, or perhaps because of, the lack of accurate reporting in the local papers. A front-page headline in the *Boston Sunday Post* explained how to avoid the grippe and warned against being "stampeded by the emphasis put upon the danger of the prevailing influenza." Instead, they offered this sage advice:

> The only persons who are likely to be affected by the germs of the disease are those . . . who are so disturbed in mind by worry or fear that they are unable to summon enough strength of body or mind to ward off the bacteria. A healthy person who exercises moderately . . . who keeps his brain clear and avoids undue fatigue is reasonably sure to have no trouble from influenza.

Again, the advice was almost completely wrong. Early in the epidemic, William Woodward, health commissioner of Boston, had identified the most troubling feature of the Spanish influenza—it was most likely to kill young adults in the prime of life. Throughout the course of its reign of terror, the death rate from the Spanish flu was heaviest in the twenty to forty age group, especially targeting vigorous young men and pregnant women.

Now, almost ninety years after the epidemic took its toll, scientists have learned how a vigorous response from a healthy immune system can turn strength into weakness and harm the body. In 1918 the population only knew that seemingly healthy people were rapidly becoming ill and dropping like flies. The Spanish influenza hit like a baseball bat. One minute you were healthy, the next minute you were desperately ill. People collapsed on the sidewalk or while riding on a trolley. In many cases people came down with symptoms, suffered miserably, and died within twelve hours.

While disease spread like wildfire in military encampments and newspapers continued to advise against being exposed to crowds, a military review was scheduled for September 15. Exercising the privilege of his new command, Maj. Gen. Henry McCain watched 20,000 men march onto the parade grounds at Camp Devens, the center of the influenza storm.

By September 15, the *Boston Herald* was able to report 2,000 cases of the flu at Camp Devens. On September 17 the *Boston Post* carried a story on page 9 that reported an increase to 3,000.

Even though the influenza had now begun to attack the civilian population, information continued to be buried on the inside pages of most papers. Even as the civilian death toll steadily climbed to forty-two per day by September 20, newspapers continued to feature headlines that the "Grippe is on the wane," that the "Grip is under control," or that increased deaths were "weather related." Contradicting their own headlines, the same editions of the same papers carried worrisome stories of desperately ill doctors and nurses at the Boston City Hospital or urgent calls for Red Cross volunteers.

Postmaster William F. Murray was largely responsible for bringing the story of the Spanish influenza to the front pages of Boston's papers. Murray had served on the Governor's Council, the Boston Common Council, and in the state legislature. At age thirty he had been one of the youngest men elected to Congress. He was, according to the *Boston Globe,* "one of the best-loved figures in the public life of Boston." His death from pneumonia brought on by the influenza was headline news on September 22. As long as the disease continued to rage, the story would no longer be absent from page 1.

By September 24, the daily death toll had climbed to eighty-seven, and the tone of the headlines had changed. Boston schools were closed. Suburban towns were finally portrayed as struggling to cope with the epidemic. Camp Devens now had more than 10,000 soldiers sick with the flu, about half of the total military personnel infected in twenty-five camps from Syracuse, New York, to Kansas and Georgia.

By the time the daily death toll in Boston reached 109, the city looked like a ghost town. With contagion all around, the public knew to stay inside. Unguarded coughing or spitting on the sidewalk became serious offenses. Relief workers handed out gauze masks—masks that we now know were largely ineffective. People understood the need to avoid sharing drinking cups and utensils. They sensed the benefits of washing their hands. In 1918, though, they had no idea that a virus sneezed into the air could infect other people for up to a day or that virus transferred from a hand to a doorknob could spread the deadly disease for as long as forty-eight hours. They didn't yet know that shutting down soda fountains was not going to do the job.

At the peak of the epidemic, the *Boston Globe* consulted Mrs. Minnie Mendelsohn of Roxbury and passed along the following cure for influenza on its front page:

Three pounds of raw onions to one pound of garlic, mix and make into a poultice. Apply this poultice to the feet, under the knees, and around the neck of the patient. Renew every three or four hours. If the lungs are affected mix a little lard in the poultice and apply.

The front page of the *Boston Post* told readers to avoid grippe danger by taking "Father John's Medicine to build fighting power. No alcohol." Other sure preventatives were egg punch, vinegar packs, and smoke from a wood fire.

As the epidemic spread large dormitories built for ship-workers in Quincy were turned into makeshift hospitals. Elsewhere, horribly sick patients spilled out of hallways onto verandas and finally into canvas tents thrown up on hospital lawns. With thirty-eight nurses sick, Boston City Hospital was closed to visitors "except in extreme emergencies." Public funerals were suspended. Bodies piled up in mortuaries and spilled out of morgues.

The draft was suspended—a drastic step in a time of war. The mayor of Boston ordered the closing of "all theatres, moving picture houses, dance halls, and all other unnecessary public assemblages." Places of worship were asked to close voluntarily.

Hundreds of nameless heroes emerged during the epidemic in Massachusetts. Selflessly, with a professional's knowledge of the certain danger, doctors and nurses risked their own lives to relieve the suffering of the desperately ill. Without effective means to cure the deadly influenza, the medical community exhausted itself doing what they could. Their ranks were steadily depleted by the very disease that they were fighting.

Henry Endicott, manager of the Massachusetts Committee of Public Safety, expressed the official view:

> The doctors and nurses of Massachusetts who are devoting themselves to the care of the sick in this emergency are all heroes and heroines and many of them have paid the penalty. Not one of them of whom I know has shirked, in any way; they are overworked, they are without sleep, and still they go on. Massachusetts can never repay its debt to this noble band of men and women.

In a proclamation in late September, the governor of Massachusetts desperately called for volunteers to fill the thinning ranks of doctors and nurses. "It is earnestly requested that everyone who has had medical or nursing experience or who can assist in any way communicate with the Commissioner of Health at the State House."

Medical and nursing students pitched in as volunteers. Most were young adults vulnerable to the disease. Many died. As the daily death toll topped 150, headlines predicted that 500 physicians and 1,000 nurses were on the way to Boston to fight the disease. With the help of the Red Cross, volunteers from as far away as Canada hurried to Massachusetts to lend their support.

The wave of death and misery peaked in Boston by early October but continued to rage through the rest of the commonwealth until early November when the worst was over. The process that created the killer disease also ended the epidemic. Completely beyond human control, the virus continued to mutate and change and simply became less deadly.

The Spanish influenza that spread from Boston in 1918 caused more deaths in less time than any other disease in the history of the human race. More than 20,000 people died in Massachusetts. Throughout the United States, the Spanish flu killed 549,000 and sickened 25 percent of the population.

CHAPTER 10

THE BATTLE OF ORLEANS

U-Boat Attack on Cape Cod
1918

Summer Sunday mornings on the beaches of Cape Cod often look like the definition of peace and quiet. Cottagers on the Cape enjoy a second cup of coffee on a porch overlooking the sea. Vacationers rise late—in no rush to begin the day's activities. Churchgoers dress in their Sunday finest and amble off toward the ringing of distant bells.

The morning of July 21, 1918, was such a morning, but folks who kept up with the news knew that all was not as it seemed. Papers of the day carried reports from General Pershing and news that the Yanks had crossed the Marne. World War I seemed far away, but recent events caused concern closer to home for people on the Cape. A British steamer and a Swedish freighter had been sunk off Nantucket. News reports were uncertain whether the ill-fated ships had struck mines left by a German U-boat or had simply been torpedoed. Fishermen were cautious, and in quiet communities on the outer Cape, some residents even secretly feared a German invasion.

Shipping lanes between New England and New York pass close to the outer Cape. By 10 A.M. on that July morning, sharp-eyed observers may have seen the large freighters *Arlington* and *J. B. King* as they passed each other in the lifting fog—one headed north, the other south.

Making its way from Gloucester to the Virginia Capes with a crew of sixteen men was the ocean-going tug *Perth Amboy* of the Lehigh Coal & Navigation Company. Captained by I. H. Tupley, the tug pulled four barges: 766 with Capt. Henry Robe, his wife, and two-man crew; 703 with Capt. Peter Peterson, his wife, daughter, and a crew of one; 740 with Capt. Joseph Perry and a three-man crew; and the barge *Lansford* with Capt. Charles Ainsleigh, his wife, and two sons.

Captains and crews navigated with care off the treacherous outer Cape, but on this day they cruised with ease through the summer haze about 4 miles off the entrance to Nauset Harbor. A deckhand on the *Perth Amboy* was the first to spot something odd. A streak in the water shot past off the stern. When two more streaks sped close by also wide of the mark, he shouted to the pilot. But the realization that three torpedoes had narrowly missed their mark came in the same instant that a gun barrel flashed off to the east at the edge of the heaviest fog.

On what would be a day of terrible marksmanship, the first shot from 2 miles away nevertheless scored a direct hit. A shell tore into the wheelhouse of the unarmed tug and caused the only serious injuries of the day. On deck, John Botovich was badly wounded when shrapnel struck his arm. John Vitz didn't know what hit him: "I was sleeping in my bunk, when 'Bang!' I woke up and half the pilot-house was gone, the tug was afire, and part of my right hand was gone."

The German submarine U-156 crept out of the fog bank and continued firing from deck guns mounted fore and aft. Shots rang out like clockwork every one or two minutes, but few found their target. Captain Tupley later observed that "the submarine fired enough shots to sink the entire Lehigh Valley fleet" and that "the fire was very erratic and the gunners seemed to be nervous."

Tupley continued: "We were powerless against such an enemy, and all that we could do was to stand there and take what they sent us. . . . I never saw a more glaring example of rotten marksmanship. Shots went wild repeatedly and but few that were fired scored hits."

With the pilothouse ablaze from the first shot, the crew of the *Perth Amboy* took to their small boats, and the U-boat turned its attention to the barges. Slowly sailing down the line of sitting ducks, the submarine shelled the barges for what turned out to be an hour and a half.

Back on shore the thunder of the firing guns confirmed the worst fears of a few Cape dwellers. The timid took to their cellars. Others were convinced that the invasion had begun. Deputy Sheriff James Boland answered his telephone with a shouted plea: "The Germans are coming after us! Hurry up and come down here and save Orleans."

Maj. Herbert L. Harris, local commander of the Cape Cod battalion of the State Guard, got on the phone and called out his troops. They gathered in the center of the village confidently ready to fend off the expected German attack.

Amos Lefavour was on his way to church with his family in a town that he thought had never been so quiet, when suddenly "like thunder" came the sound of shots from the direction of the sea. At first, Lefavour said, "All seemed to think that the dreaded, expected . . . bombardment of the cape had started," but, he concluded, "Cape Cod has met the German submarine menace and is not afraid."

More typically, vacationers and residents alike rallied to the beach for a firsthand glimpse of the excitement. As the *Boston Post* explained it:

> No moving picture manager could have staged a sea battle more effectively for the thousands of summer visitors in this vicinity. Bathers taking their morning dip scurried ashore when shells splashed within a few hundred yards of them and watched the German exhibition of frightfulness without fear, but with keen excitement from the beach.

While as many as an estimated 1,000 spectators flocked to Nauset Heights for a view of the battle, cottagers, according to the *Post*, "did not have to move from their piazza chairs to see every detail of the little drama."

The drama played out with the German submarine repeatedly firing at the helpless barges one by one. It was not until the U-boat crept to within a few hundred yards of the barges that the shelling finally took its toll.

With the tug *Perth Amboy* ablaze and barge 703 heading for the ocean bottom, a hero emerged on the *Lansford*, the fourth and final barge. Frustrated by the lack of weapons with which to return fire, Jack Ainsleigh, the twelve-year-old son of the *Lansford*'s captain, knew he had to do something. Rushing below decks, he grabbed his American flag with every intention of sending the submarine crew a message.

As Captain Ainsleigh told the *Boston Globe:*

My little boy Jack appeared to enjoy the whole affair and his display of courage is truly remarkable. As soon as the shells began coming toward us he insisted that he get his American flag which was in the cabin. I told him he had better get his things together and get ready to get into the boat, but instead . . . [he] got his American flag, and standing there on the deck defiantly waved the flag in the face of the German commander.

Fortunately for Jack, the aim of the German crew did not improve, though they did manage to put five holes in the Lansford, which settled at the bow.

As a flotilla of small lifeboats from the tug and four barges slowly made its way toward shore, the submarine fired shells in their direction. Undaunted, young Jack continued to stand and wave his flag all the way in to shore. Crowds on the beach, photographers, and reporters all responded to the boy's pluck with a rousing cheer and a huge reception. He was rewarded with pictures and front-page headlines in virtually all of the Boston papers.

Seeing the precarious circumstances that the lifeboats faced, Clarence P. Robbin and Lawrence Hopkins put out in their lobster boat and helped tow the smaller boats to shore. Cottagers and vacationers welcomed the flotilla on the beach in spite of intermittent shells that flew over their heads.

Giuseppi Massetti, a fisherman, had just returned to port when he saw the first shell hit American soil.

There was a spurt of flame, a puff of smoke, then a sort of shrieking, whining noise, and next I saw sand flying in all directions a few hundred yards on my left. I started towards the spot. There I saw a deep hole as though a steam shovel had gouged out a cellar.

According to the *Boston Post,* Mrs. Weston Taylor was working in her kitchen when another shot came whizzing by.

> It seemed as though a gigantic sky-rocket went over the house. There was a great hissing and sizzling sound. I had heard the shot and I at once suspected that it was a shell from a submarine. It did not seem to be more than a few feet above the roof of the house. I rushed out to see where the shot had struck and found that it had landed in some water.

Miss Evelyn Ham and several other young women were swimming in Meeting House Pond when the same shell Mrs. Weston saw livened up their morning. Whistling just a few feet above their heads, the shell hit with a great splash just a few hundred yards from the spot where they were bathing. They weren't very frightened and managed to joke about it— later on.

The commotion at sea and along the beach finally attracted the attention of the Chatham Naval Air Station just a few miles down the shore. The *Boston Globe* brusquely reported what proved to be a nonevent:

> Three airplanes were dispatched from the Chatham Naval Air Station, the aviators being supplied with bombs. The airplanes hovered over the U-boat and dropped bombs. The submarine returned the fire. Neither side registered a hit.

In fact, as explained with apparent disgust by the *Boston Transcript,* the bombs were duds:

> Airplanes from Chatham dropped two bombs near enough the German submarine off Orleans yesterday to sink or disable it, but the bombs failed to explode. In this connection it is reported that ammunition furnished in this district is notoriously unreliable. . . . [T]his alone saved the enemy craft from destruction or from damage that would have made its capture easy.

Nevertheless, the appearance of the Navy planes may have had the desired effect. Whether due to exhaustion from hours of shooting or from fear that the planes might drop a bomb that was not a dud, the U-boat soon submerged and was last seen heading south.

After the shooting ended other stories surfaced in the local papers. The skipper of the fishing boat *Rosie,* out of Boston on a seining trip, claimed to have seen the attack on the tug and barges. The U-boat "looked like a big whale with the water sparkling in the sunlight as it rolled off her sides," before one of the deck guns turned toward the *Rosie.* When a shell "came skipping along the water," said the captain, "I yelled for Tony down below for full speed ahead, and the way the *Rosie* jumped ahead through the brine made me feel a little more comfortable."

When all was said and done, the German U-boat partially burned a tug that eventually would be salvaged, sank two empty barges, damaged a third empty barge, and sank one barge loaded with granite. News accounts developed a theme comparing the cost of the tug and barges with the cost of the ammunition that the Germans fired. The consensus was that during the Battle of Orleans the German submarine had wasted more money in ammunition than their helpless targets were worth.

The official response was one of curious surprise. Why would a German sub waste so much time on insignificant non-military targets? Navy commanders were also amazed that a submarine would dare to operate in the treacherous waters of the outer cape. Perhaps summing up the official view, the *Boston Transcript* explained:

> The German commander either took a long chance or had an exact chart of the dangerous shoals and shifting sandbars off the Cape. It would be impossible for him to submerge to any great depth and the scene of his exploits was not one in which under-sea boats might be expected to operate.

And Rear Adm. Spencer Wood provided the most official explanation of the U-boat's activities when he called it a ridiculous stunt, designed to impress the German people and part of a campaign to excite the American people—what today we might call terrorism. Not a man to mince words, Admiral Wood had some final thoughts:

> Incidentally, if the German sea fighters are of the impression that this kind of four-flush tactics will terrify the American people they have a lot to learn of the sentiment of this country. Such foolish and futile demonstrations have quite the opposite effect for they assure the people rather than terrify them.

CHAPTER 11

A STICKY SITUATION

The Great Molasses Flood

1919

In January 1919 Massachusetts joined the rest of the world in breathing a sigh of relief. Only months before, the great war in Europe had finally ended. Navy ships were sailing home from across the sea, and soldiers and sailors were getting ready to return to civilian life.

In Boston's busy harbor the navy training ship *Nantucket* was docked at Battery Wharf within sight of the Charlestown Navy Yard. Along Commercial Street in the North End, freight terminals hummed with peacetime activity. Another 600,000 gallons of molasses had just arrived by ship from Cuba and was added to the huge storage tank of the Purity Distilling Company, a subsidiary of the United States Industrial Alcohol Company. Located on the waterfront side of Commercial Street close to the North End Playground, the 100-by-40-foot container held 2,300,000 gallons of molasses that was to eventually find its way to the company's plant in Cambridge.

Ironically, on a mild winter day in mid-January, newspapers headlines screamed with predictions of the coming of national prohibition. Only one more state was needed in the "dry" column to ratify a constitutional amendment that would put distillers out of business.

At noontime on January 15, many people were taking the time to enjoy the beautiful weather and bask in a newly restored sense of well-being. Robert Burnett, who lived on Commercial Street, was at home eating dinner with his family. Ralph Martin and Dave Spellman were lounging in the park sitting on an automobile. Bridgett Clougherty, her daughter Theresa, and her son Stephen were having lunch in their dining room at 6 Copps Hill Terrace, while her son Martin, who worked nights, slept in the next room.

The mood was mellow in business establishments too. William White, custodian of the giant molasses tank, took the noon hour off to meet his wife for a luncheon and shopping. At freight house number 4 of the Boston & Worcester Street Railway Company, freight agent Dorley worked with a short crew of three clerks in a small office above the warehouse.

In a nearby firehouse attached to fireboat 31, several men were quietly passing the time. Hoseman William H. Connor, just home from serving on the USS *Kearsarge,* was playing cards with Nat Bowering, Patrick Driscoll, Frank McDermott, and George Lahey in the recreation room of the firehouse. One of the firemen remarked what a quiet day it had been with no alarm all morning. Too quiet, Lahey thought, like something was about to break.

Outside, horses pulling freight wagons lumbered along the streets. Children from neighborhood tenements bid their mothers good-bye, heading back to school after the midday recess. Workmen stopped for conversations, and a street railway train rattled past on its elevated tracks just to the west of the giant molasses tank.

Most witnesses agreed that the first sign of trouble was an ominous rumbling sound—not the bang of an explosion. The cause of the disaster would long be debated, but whether tank failure or explosion, it made little difference to the results. Shattering the midday calm, the giant tank ruptured with such unbelievable force that its three-quarter-inch steel sides blasted into the elevated street railway tracks. As described by the *Boston Post*, which provided extensive coverage of the disaster, the tank "smote the huge steel girders of the 'L' structure and bent and twisted and snapped them as if by the smash of a giant fist." The elevated tracks were obliterated for more than 100 feet.

Each gallon of thick molasses weighed 11¾ pounds. In the blink of an eye, as much as twenty-seven million pounds of molasses was on the loose. A tidal wave 30 feet or higher gushed toward the tenements and houses on Copps Hill Terrace. After the wave washed up against the strong brick structures at the base of the hill, it swirled with deadly force back toward the harbor.

Robert Burnett told the *Post:*

> I thought it was an elevated train, until I heard a swish as if the wind was rushing. Then it became dark. I looked out the windows [from a second-floor dining room] and saw this great black wave coming. It didn't rush. It just rolled, slowly it seemed, like the side of a mountain falling into space. Of course, it came quickly. . . . We snatched open the door of the hall and molasses

was already at the top of the 14 step flight of stairs. I slammed the door and we ran for the roof.

At 6 Copps Hill Terrace, Martin Clougherty woke when he heard a slight rumble, "and could see nothing but blackness all around with a few flashes of light." He said, "I seemed to be smothering when [all] of a sudden I got a breath of fresh air. I did not know where I was. I thought I was in the water. . . . I found what turned out to be a part of my house resting on my chest."

Martin's mother, Bridgett Clougherty, was killed according to the *Boston Post,* "when she was blown through the walls of her home and buried under the debris of her dwelling."

Martin McDonough, who occupied another apartment in the same building, remembered only hearing a crash as he was about to eat a bite of mashed potatoes. He was found unconscious in the street. The entire building was demolished when the tidal wave of molasses swept it 100 feet off its foundation.

At the freight office, agent Dorley had his first impression confirmed.

We were sitting there at work, when there came the sound of a rumble. Instinctively I knew what it was. "Molasses tank gone," I cried. The words were barely out when the avalanche came. We heard the crash of the steel tank as it hurtled to the ground. The broken parts of the tank missed our shed only by a matter of inches. . . . Parts of the tank struck other houses and they were crumpled like eggs. . . . We were trapped in the office. Beneath us surged the flood, sweeping everything before it. Men and horses about in the yard

An 8-foot molasses wave killed many people and destroyed much of Boston's North End when a two-million-gallon tank of molasses burst in 1919.

COURTESY OF THE BOSTON PUBLIC LIBRARY, PRINT DEPARTMENT

were caught up and tossed here and there like so many logs in a torrent.

As in many disasters luck played a part in deciding who was to live and who was to die. A patrolman walking his beat felt some liquid splash against the back of his uniform but was able to duck around a corner before the force of the wave hit. A sailor chatting with a pretty girl on the street felt himself swept away and slightly injured. The girl was among the missing. In North End Park, Dave Spellman watched as the wave of sticky goo washed his friend Ralph Martin into the harbor.

A workman unloading a load of lard was severely injured and his horse killed when the wave of molasses struck his delivery wagon. An oil tanker was completely demolished, and a teamster loading a wagon at the street railway terminal was thrown to the pavement and his horse and wagon crushed. Two girls, age nine and eleven, didn't return to school for the afternoon and were presumed missing in the carnage.

Most deaths in the mayhem were the result of asphyxiation. As the *Boston Post* again explained:

> There was no escape from the wave. Caught, human being and animal alike could not flee. Running in it was impossible. Snared in its flood was to be stifled. Once it smeared a head—human or animal—there was no coughing off the sticky mass. To attempt to wipe it with hands was to make it worse. . . . It plugged nostrils almost airtight.

Lt. Cdr. William Copeland was on the upper deck of the training ship *Nantucket* when he saw the tank burst. Within five minutes his crew rushed to the scene with stretchers, first-aid kits, and the manpower needed to rescue survivors. From the Charlestown Navy Yard, Commander Rush sent crews from the mine sweepers *Starling, Breaker,* and *Billow,* which were anchored off the North End pier. Two navy tugs and a submarine chaser hurried to the scene, an army hospital in Roxbury sent a medical detachment of eighty men, and support services were provided by the Boston Red Cross.

What the rescuers found was an absolute mess. Reeking molasses, waist deep percolated through the scattered ruins of houses, freight terminals, wagons, and railroad cars that had been splintered and smashed by the heavy tide. Here and there signs of submerged thrashing suggested a life, but whether it was horse or human was impossible to tell. The sludge was so sticky and thick that medical personnel at local hospitals could not immediately determine the gender of rescued survivors. Slopping onto the floor, the thick sludge fouled the wheels of hospital gurneys.

Wading through slick tangles of unseen debris, rescuers risked their own safety in the flowing mess. Rubber boots were a hindrance filling as they did with heavy molasses. Some rescuers could be seen in stocking feet chopping away wreckage with fire axes or cutting through metal with acetylene torches.

On a day filled with heroic efforts, the longest, most harrowing, and most desperate rescue attempt occurred at the firehouse of fireboat 31. George Lahey had just left the card game and was heading upstairs to check on the fireboat when the tide of molasses hit. With astounding power the tide actually lifted the firehouse, which topped out at three and a half stories, and dropped it to the ground again. The concussion threw Lahey back down the stairs onto the floor of the recreation room.

Molasses and pieces of metal tank crashing through the building overturned a massive slate pool table, which pinned Lahey to the floor and against a wall.

Meanwhile, before the impact hoseman William Connor saw a wall of molasses that looked to him to be 150 feet high and approaching as fast as a cyclone. "Jump quick," he yelled, and Patrick Driscoll dove head first through the nearest window. But Connor and Nat Bowering, along with Lahey, were not as lucky. Knocked onto the floor, they were trapped in the wrecked building when the second story collapsed.

As Connor later remembered:

> The second floor was held from crushing us to death by only a few chairs and the piano. I was lying on my back. There was scarcely 18 inches between me and the second floor. We knew that if anyone came in on the floor above we would be killed instantly.

But the three men quickly discovered that being crushed to death was the least of their worries. The building had narrowly escaped being washed into the harbor. Stuck at the edge of the dock, the ruined building that held the three trapped men was directly in the path of thousands of gallons of heavy molasses that were determined to flow down to the water.

Trapped on their backs in a narrow opening, the men suddenly recognized their real danger. The incessant flood of molasses carried flotillas of wreckage as it flowed into their prison. The floating debris continually clogged the single small hole at the far end that let the ooze escape toward the harbor.

Connor was able to grab hold of Lahey's foot, which stuck through a partition that separated them. "For God's sake, help me," Lahey pleaded. "This stuff will soon be up to my neck. For God's sake get help or we'll die."

But Connor was stuck himself.

Realizing that we would be drowned like rats in a trap if the outlet were not kept open, I crawled to the opening and with my legs kicked the pieces of board from the hole. . . . It seemed weeks that we laid there. The flood of molasses at times flowed up to our ears. We bumped our heads on the floor above always trying to keep our nose and mouth above the fluid.

Finally, after about thirty minutes, a ranger from the *Nantucket* saw Connor's foot moving in the ruins. It was the start of a frantic two-hour effort. Never thinking of themselves, a team of sailors smashed the clogged outlet and crawled into the trap. With saws and muscle they tore away the beams that imprisoned Bowering and Connor. The sailors pulled the two men to safety. But Lahey still remained.

Desperately cutting away a portion of the wooden floor beneath him, rescuers were able to make contact with the trapped fireman. With Lahey's weakening voice directing their efforts, a team of fifty rangers then had to wield acetylene torches to cut away the iron and steel that held Lahey down.

But it was too late. The arduous rescue had taken too long. In the final minutes before the sailors reached the fireman's body, Lahey had lost consciousness. Unable to hold himself up, Lahey's head drooped and he drowned.

The great molasses flood killed twenty-one people and injured another 150. Crews spent months spraying the area with fire hoses to clean the sticky liquid from the cobblestone streets of the North End.

Litigation took years. The distilling company argued that some outside force had caused their tank to explode. In the end, though, most people came to believe that the tank was just not strong enough to contain its humongous load. The company paid nearly $1 million in claims.

WASHED AWAY

The Failure of the Wheeler Dam

1927

For people who liked small towns, Becket was almost idyllic. Nestled in the hills of western Massachusetts about 12 miles southeast of Pittsfield, Becket (not to be confused with Becket Center) was a tidy village of about 700 souls who prospered in their isolation. Settled next to a stream that ran close to Main Street, Becket began its existence as a typical mill town. Snuggled in a small valley between cloistering wooded slopes, the village made its mark with manufacturing rather than agriculture. Dams and reservoirs sprouted all over town, providing valuable waterpower to its thriving mills and factories. In the words of the *Berkshire Evening Eagle,* in 1927 "Becket was . . . the sole remaining typical old Berkshire industrial village."

In some ways, however, Becket was unique. A progressive little town, Becket had the foresight to change with changing times, yet retained the heart of a small village. People in Becket took care of each other and shared a real regard for their friends and neighbors.

At one time a tannery had been the biggest business in town, but the tannery fell on hard times. The factory and the original dam that held its reservoir fell into disrepair. But Becket bounced back. Monroe Ballou replaced the Wheeler Dam back around 1882, and then one of his sons ran a basket shop that used its waterpower. A fashionable silk mill replaced the old tannery. Everyone in town had a job, and soon the little village of Becket became a center of employment.

The Berkshire and Becket Silk Mill grew so fast that eighty people were employed there. Most of the workers were women who commuted each day on the Boston & Albany Railroad. The Ballou brothers added a second basket shop and gave jobs to thirty-three people. Clinton Ballou put even more men to work at four portable sawmills and a gristmill owned by the family. In addition the C. E. Lyman sawmill employed as many as eight men all year long, and Roy Smith's brand-new silk mill was just getting started.

All of these mills and factories, of course, needed the support of retail stores. Leon Harris and his wife lived above his general store. Raymond's market, another small shop, the post office, and the telephone building were all to be found scattered between private homes and a few tenements that fronted on Main Street.

By 1927 no large public utility had extended electrical power to Becket. But that didn't stop the town. Each night, the old-fashioned kerosene street lamps along Main Street were lighted. Every dawn, they were extinguished. In the meantime homes with what the *Eagle* described as "private electrical plants" were quietly running wires for lights. Here and there as you passed through the village, you could already spot the bright electric glow of the town's promising future.

Rain came early and often in the fall of 1927. Already soaked to the bone, cloudbursts on November 3 brought death-dealing floods to much of New England. The hill towns of western Massachusetts and Vermont suffered the most. The Hoosac River ran down the middle of Main Street in North Adams. Pittsfield and scattered towns throughout the Berkshires were isolated by washed-out highways, railroads, and telephone lines. The broad Connecticut River put parts of Springfield and Northampton underwater in the worst flood in their history up to that time. In and around Montpelier in the river valley towns of Vermont, eighty-four people died.

The village of Becket was also hit hard. The Brooker Hill Bridge on the highway to Pittsfield was washed out, and mud-slides covered the road on the outskirts of town not far from the Lyman sawmill. Worst of all, the gentle stream that usually ran through the village had swollen so large that it washed away a section of track of the Boston & Albany Railroad. Crews struggled throughout the night to turn the course of the still-swollen stream and try to repair the railway damage.

Heavy downpours always put the village of Becket on edge. No one in Becket was more on edge than Clinton Ballou. Clint was one of the selectmen in town and the owner of the Wheeler Dam. An old-style earth-filled dam, the structure that held back fifty acres of reservoir water less than 2 miles above the town was 30 feet high and 200 feet across. On the down-stream side the dam had a vertical stone face. Behind the downstream wall, dirt, rock, and gravel were piled about 50 feet thick at the bottom and 16 feet thick at the top.

Cloudbursts and heavy rain made Clint Ballou as nervous as a cat. Especially after hours of mudslides and washed-out tracks, Clint didn't get much sleep. Anxiously driving up the hill to the dam, he checked its condition, watched the water level, and adjusted the water's flow through the floodgate. Perhaps a part of his mind kept thinking about the official findings in the recent biannual dam inspection report: "The slight bulge in the wall mentioned in the 1925 report had not increased at the time of the 1927 inspection and was not considered a source of danger." Still, Clint knew, and the people of Becket knew, that a forty-five-year-old earth-filled dam gave the town a legitimate reason to worry.

No one knows how much rain fell on Becket during the night of November 3, and the early morning hours of November 4, but nearly 7 inches were recorded in Worcester. Seven streams draining steep surrounding hills flowed into the Wheeler reservoir. Rudd Pond was even higher in the hills. Any overflow from Rudd Pond's dam also made its way to the Wheeler reservoir and put more pressure on the Wheeler Dam.

Harry Heaphy was an experienced engineer and the man who inspected the Wheeler Dam. He believed that a cloudburst in the middle of the night caused a mudslide on the far side of the mountain. On the Becket side the waters "went into Rudd Pond causing that to overflow and send a huge quantity of water into the Wheeler reservoir."

Alfred Crochiere went along with Clinton Ballou to check on the Wheeler Dam in the middle of that rain-soaked night. As they walked along the soggy crest, they saw what they had always secretly feared. A crack had appeared on the top of the dam. The only way a crevasse like that could open, they knew, was if water was seeping down below through the earth that filled the dam.

In spite of the danger, Crochiere and Ballou ran down to the small gatehouse at the base of the leaking dam. All they could do was relieve pressure on the dam by releasing water as fast as they could. They needed to be sure that the gate was open.

Creaking and groaning sounds met the two men when they burst through the gatehouse door. They checked the gate and bolted out of the building about thirty seconds before water from the leaking dam caused the gatehouse to collapse. Lucky to be alive, both men were now certain that the worst disaster Becket could imagine was about to happen. It was 4:30 A.M.

They pounded on the door of the first house they came to directly below the dam. Robert Burnham quickly phoned P. B. McCormick who ran the telephone exchange in town. Believing that he was working directly in the path of a tidal wave, McCormick began to call every telephone in Becket. Meanwhile, Ballou and Crochiere hopped in their car and raced to the village to spread the warning.

Rev. C. I. Ramsay, the pastor in Becket, was awakened by someone pounding on his door at 5 A.M. "The dam is breaking," a messenger yelled. "Get to high ground!"

"Summoning the rest of the family," the pastor later told reporters, "we quickly dressed, I got out the car, and we drove to the top of a nearby hill."

The pastor and his family joined other people from Becket who waited in the hills for the horrible flood. They waited but nothing happened. "Within an hour we began to get cold and as everything was quiet we returned to the house for breakfast," Reverend Ramsay later explained to a reporter.

Clint Ballou was puzzled too. Could he have been so wrong? Clint piled back into his car with several of his friends from town. Clint drove Howard, Smith, P. H. Tobin, Frank

LaMontague, and Albert Jacobs back up the road toward the reservoir to see if the dam was really bursting.

Water was running down the road as they sped to within sight of the dam. Clint later told an interviewer:

> I saw the water starting to break through, and turning my automobile around in the highway which already had become flooded I raced the flood to the village and beat it by about 10 minutes. That ride was one which was surrounded by danger at all times. I never drove a car so fast in all my life. I blew the horn of the machine continually and here and there saw people rushing from their homes and into their automobiles to make their way to the hills. The roads leading to the highlands in that section were well filled.

Reverend Ramsay was one of the residents of Becket who got the second message. He told the *Berkshire Evening Eagle:*

> Just as the oatmeal and coffee were ready another summons came from the outside that the dam had given way and to hurry. We quickly put on our wraps and had hardly gotten half way up the hill when we heard a great roar.
>
> Like an avalanche there appeared what seemed to be a cloud of black smoke bordered with white foam and at the base a seething white, 20 or 25 feet high. Here and there a great root would stick out for an instant only to be sucked in again. With irresistible force it crumpled house after house like matches.

When he was sure that everyone had been alerted, Clint Ballou and his friends drove to high ground at the last moment.

Standing there on the hillside I watched the waters rush down upon the village, sweeping away everything within reach. My mill went down as though it were a pile of boy's blocks. My business and my house gone. "There goes $60,000 worth of buildings, machinery, and furniture," I remarked to my friends.

While most of the people in town stood in the hills and watched the devastation, P. B. McCormick stuck to his job at the telephone exchange. Even as the flood carried away the church next door and mud, debris, and rushing water washed across the floor at his feet, McCormick continued to work the switchboard. When he couldn't link all of the residents on a party line, he kept at this task and warned every customer in the path of the flood, one by one.

Still, McCormick wasn't done. He waded out of his office and found lines that were still standing. The *Berkshire Evening Eagle* reported that "to get information to the outside world [McCormick] spliced wires to a pole a short distance from the business section, and communicated with the Pittsfield office of the New England Telephone and Telegraph Company."

The destruction of Main Street was almost complete. Two silk mills, the lumber mill, a basket shop, and the gristmill—representing virtually all of the manufacturing jobs in town—were swept off the face of the earth. The butcher shop and all of the retail stores were washed away. The post office was destroyed. In all twenty-eight buildings, including private homes and tenements, simply ceased to exist.

For a few minutes, the narrow stream that once roamed through town turned into a monster. The crushing wall of water altered the course of the stream by 65 to 75 feet and turned what used to be Main Street into a yawning chasm. A trench as wide as 100 yards, 25 feet deep, and hundreds of feet long now gaped in the heart of the village.

The fury of the water was so intense that little remained of the buildings that were hit. Wood and bricks were carried away along with much of the soil beneath the structures. Main Street was reduced to bedrock. More than 3 miles of track of the Boston & Albany Railroad were torn away. About half a dozen bridges were washed out, including one that was pushed aside in the center of town. Suddenly, the state highway ended at an abyss.

Like many others, Dr. Hugh Heaton lost his home, but he didn't mourn the loss of mere money. He told the *Berkshire Evening Eagle:*

> The loss of articles which cannot be replaced cannot be estimated. I had medals awarded me during my service in France during the world war and they are gone. At my place nothing remains but a lone maple tree. Replacing the well is a mound of dirt and debris. Five bricks from the chimney lie on the turf indicating where the house was.

The Willises, a couple who were both over eighty years old and had lived in their home for decades, refused to run to high ground. If the flood was going to take their house, it would just have to take them as well. They stayed in their house and watched the water rise. A surging river flooded their yard, shook the foundation, and piled debris against the walls, but the house and the elderly couple ultimately survived.

Mrs. Justine Carroll, the elderly housekeeper in Arthur Higley's home, had also heard the warnings, but she refused to leave the house. Remarkably, Mrs. Carroll's was the only life lost in the massive demolition of the village of Becket. Oddly, she was not drowned. After her body was recovered days later about a mile down the valley, authorities found that she had died of a broken neck. She was killed, they believe, by falling beams when the massive wall of water demolished the Higley house.

One day after the flood, the *Berkshire Evening Eagle* reported that Becket "looked like a bit of the world war." The Red Cross flag flew from a staff at the town hall. "State troopers galore swarmed the town. . . . Planes hovered in the air, and large crowds attempted to reach the center of town. There is little actual suffering in town. The Red Cross is effectively caring for the situation at present."

Just twenty-four hours after the flood, cots, blankets, and food arrived in Becket, together with a military field kitchen. Martial law was declared so the state police could keep out looters. Eight telephone lines were up and working within two days. Transportation officials immediately dispatched steam shovels and highway trucks to fix the state highway and fill in the Becket chasm. Buses arrived with 200 men to rebuild miles of railroad track. A relief fund started in Pittsfield collected thousands of dollars to restore the town. The basket factory shifted its work to another building, and the owner of Raymond's store found a red barn still standing on solid footings that made a perfect meat market.

Public discussions addressed plans to bring in electrical power to service new mills that would replace the missing structures. People in town were upbeat and resilient. It would take much more than a burst dam and a tidal wave to wipe Becket off the map.

CHAPTER 13

WATER OVER THE DAM

The Connecticut River Floods

1936

On March 10, 1936, the *Springfield Daily News* ran a small headline at the top of its Northampton section: "An Abundant Water Supply Is Indicated." For readers in old mill towns in an agricultural region, the story was meant as serious news. Rain and melting snow were rapidly raising the water level in Northampton's Mountain Street reservoir. "The situation forecasts an abundant supply for the summer," the paper reported.

Just two days later, residents learned the hard way that the region's supply of water was way beyond abundant.

The Connecticut River comes to life in the pine forests of New Hampshire, separates the states of Vermont and New Hampshire, and divides the Commonwealth of Massachusetts before sweeping through Connecticut on its way to the sea. During the long, cold winter of 1936, the Connecticut and its many tributaries froze hard into sheets of ice. The late winter rains of early March broke open New England's rivers and set the ice free in a matter of days. What people didn't realize was that much of that ice was headed for a bridge just a little downstream of Northampton.

By Friday, March 13, the *Springfield Daily News* ran far different headlines on its front page: "Scores Flee Homes in Northampton, Driven Out by Huge Ice Blockade." Carried by the rising water, massive amounts of broken ice caught on the bridge that crossed the Connecticut River at Mount Tom Junction. In short order thick cakes of ice, 18 feet high and a mile long, piled up across the width of the broad river.

At Mount Tom the level of the river was actually higher than the highway that ran beside it, but the river was held in check for a time by the raised roadbed of the Boston & Maine railway. As huge chunks of river ice were thrown to within 2 feet of the railroad tracks, homes on the other side were abandoned for fear that the railroad "dike" would soon burst.

Upstream in the "meadows" section of Northampton, the damage was already done. Six hours before the river was expected to peak, the *Springfield Daily News* reported that the rich river-bottom land of the meadows "had been transformed into a vast ice-dotted lake. Farm houses in low lying sections were under water to the second floor. Similar scenes were noted on the Hadley side of the river where a large area is inundated."

In a cottage near the banks of the river in Hatfield, Joseph Eberlin and Walter Walsh turned in the night before without a care. They awoke in the middle of the night to find their home surrounded by floodwater. They yelled for help, and a fellow townsman, Michael Gogel, rescued them at dawn in his canoe.

Northampton's Mayor, Charles Dunn, fumed at the lack of action to break up the immense jam and complained about the

Tobacco fields near Northampton destroyed by the 1936 Connecticut River flood.
LIBRARY OF CONGRESS, PRINTS & PHOTOGRAPHS DIVISION, FSA/OWI COLLECTION, LC-USF33-010040-M4

lack of regard shown to the citizens of his city. By the night of March 15, though, ice on the eastern edge of the river began to slip downstream. By the next morning much of the jam had dispersed and the crisis had clearly passed.

On March 18, headlines in the *Boston Post* announced that the "Menace of High Water Is Passing." But sharp-eyed readers may have been troubled by the details of the story. Torrents of rain had fallen for twenty hours in northern New Hampshire. Near its headwaters the mighty Connecticut River was 12 feet above its normal height and flooding New Hampshire towns.

The menace of high water had not passed. Massachusetts had only seen the first act. From the mid-Atlantic to all of New England, mid-March of 1936 brought rain that fell in buckets

for several days. In hindsight the incredible floods that hammered all of Massachusetts and much of the East Coast were
caused by extraordinary conditions in northern New England.
G. Harold Noyes, the chief weather forecaster for New England
at the time, attributed the flooding to over 20 inches of rain
that fell in the White Mountains, which melted another 20
inches of snow pack. For cities and towns in Massachusetts, it
was just a matter of days before a devastating flood arrived.

Newspapers in western Massachusetts were closer to the
mayhem. Unlike the Boston papers, their headlines told of
sudden widespread disaster. "Death, Damage, Misery"
screamed the *Berkshire County Eagle* when the Hoosac River
ran a foot deep on Ashmand Street, Adams's main thoroughfare, and every bridge in North Adams was in danger of washing away. The *Worcester Evening Gazette* told of the Nashua
River rampaging over its banks in the town of Fitchburg, spoke
of torrents in the streets of Webster, and reported that the force
of the water was blowing off manhole covers throughout the
city of Worcester.

In the midst of statewide devastation, the hardest hit areas
were still in the towns that lined the Connecticut River. From
Greenfield, Deerfield, Hatfield, and Hadley to Northampton,
Holyoke, Springfield, and Chicopee, the frigid waters were rising. For the second time in a week, the meadows section of
Northampton was again underwater, but this time the rest of
the city was flooded too. Homeowners packed their posses-
sions. Refugees fled by the hundreds. The entire city was isolated when the bridge to Hadley was closed. In Westfield, the
Westfield River was rising at the rate of 2 feet per hour.
Residents of West Springfield evacuated hours before a dike
broke and their homes were inundated.

And the rivers kept rising. Most early news reports compared the floods with the horrible deluge of 1927. The Agawam River was within 6 inches of the 1927 mark, threatening already flooded Northampton. Holyoke was taking precautions in the event the river rose like it did in 1927.

But the rivers kept rising. When all was said and done, the flood of 1936 shattered records set just nine years before. Water at the Holyoke Dam exceeded the prior record by more than two feet. At the Memorial Bridge in Springfield, water passed the old mark by 4 feet and still continued to rise. At Turners Falls the power company reported that 235,000 cubic feet of water per second were pounding over the dam—well beyond the 172,000 cubic feet measured in 1927.

The results were catastrophic. Highways and rail lines were quickly submerged and severed. Motorists were stranded, and 300 passengers waited for canceled trains at Springfield's Union Station. Throughout western Massachusetts bridges were washed away at a wholesale rate. Towns and cities were isolated. Homes and factories were flooded and power stations closed. Springfield, Northampton, Holyoke, and Chicopee were not only inundated but also left in the dark. In Northampton alone 6 square miles were flooded for a period of four days. Water in Springfield spread over an area of 8 square miles. The *Springfield Daily News* reported that practically the entire town of Hadley was underwater, and most residents were removed to the town hall, where for the time being they were stranded.

Desperate efforts were being made to rescue a number of persons trapped in their homes by flood waters at Hatfield. Water five feet deep was running through the

center of town. . . . Approximately 200 persons were
known to be marooned on Wheeling Island, a community of 10,000 persons where only the highest church
steeple and the roofs and upper floors of the higher
buildings showed above the flood waters.

As bad as the conditions were, people who resided all
along the Connecticut River lived under the cloud of a worse
fear. Just north of the Massachusetts border, the huge Vernon
Dam, which supplied electric power to the region, stretched
across the Connecticut River. At the peak of the March flood, a
"head" of 28 feet of water poured over the top of the massive
dam. In spite of newspaper headlines that claimed that the
Vernon Dam had "gone out," more than one hundred workers
and National Guardsmen "worked like titans" in drenching
rain to sandbag the dam abutments to keep them from washing out. Failure was not an option. A breach of the Vernon
Dam would unleash a wall of water that would sweep away
whole communities where hundreds of thousands of people
lived.

"The dam hasn't gone out and it isn't going to go out,"
declared the superintendent of the Vernon Dam. "The power
house has been abandoned, but the dam still holds, and we
have plugged a hole that developed." Still, residents of the
Connecticut River Valley stood watch throughout the night in
shifts of two or three hours. The *Springfield Daily News*
reported that "river populations were haggard after a night of
sleepless horror, made the worse by scores of terrifying rumors
of broken dams and walls of water."

In Springfield and North Adams and many towns in
between, the National Guard was mobilized to lend a hand.

Cots, blankets, emergency food, generators, searchlights, and medical supplies were rushed to the flooded region. Guardsmen sealed off bridges and streets that were too dangerous to cross, and in cities like Springfield, the guard began to police the streets after declarations of martial law.

All hands were needed to man the barricades against the invading water. Seven hundred men fought in Holyoke in a futile effort to bolster a 20-foot dike. More than 63,000 sandbags were piled high to save the Holyoke Dam. At bridges, dikes, dams, and power stations along the Connecticut River and its many tributaries, thousands of police, guardsmen, CCC workers, and civilian volunteers struggled in a desperate effort to save whatever they could.

Hundreds of men, women, and children huddled on rooftops in the stricken area. But, of course, unlike more recent hurricane and flood scenes from New Orleans in 2005, helicopters were not available to rescue victims in 1936.

People responded as best they could. An Amherst banker, Mr. R. O. Moody, and his son piled into their rowboat and saved eighteen residents of Hadley. But returning to shore on their last trip with a cargo of three other men, the rowboat capsized in the turbulent water. Moody and his son grabbed onto an apple tree and hung there from midnight to 4 A.M., when they hopped on a passing log. A short shuttle on an ice cake got them to a small island, where they were rescued at 6:30 A.M. Two of their passengers were also saved, but William McGrath of Hadley became the first Massachusetts fatality in the flood. The swirling river swept him away. He left a wife and five children who already had been evacuated.

The need for boats was desperate and the call was answered from afar. Gloucester fishermen from Gorton-Pew fisheries and the Atlantic Supply Company notified Governor Curley that they and their dories would leave at once for any area. The Coast Guard volunteered twenty crewmen, and seventy sailors from the Charlestown Navy Yard also were dispatched to Northampton. Surfboats from the lifesaving stations at Nahant and Point Atherton were loaded onto trucks and rushed to North Hadley, along with twenty men and four dories. Fifty trucks carried private boats donated by families from Marblehead, Gloucester, and other seaside towns. Last but not least, the Goldstein brothers provided all the boats and canoes at the Stillwater Canoe Club, and the state's Public Safety Commissioner Paul Kirk ordered the purchase of a twenty-six-foot power boat with a 125-horsepower motor.

The boatmen had their hands full. Donald Bean, a graduate student at Massachusetts State College, unsuccessfully tried to get to class by walking a plank across a gap in a railroad bridge above the Connecticut River. Clinging to bushes in ten feet of water, 2 miles from any assistance, he was rescued almost four hours later.

Mrs. Felix Lebrun refused to leave her Springfield cottage even though, as the *Boston Post* reported, "the ice-flecked river literally roared through her back yard."

"I am not going to give up the ship," said the elderly woman. "I have lived here all my life and I love it." She watched the neighborhood children wrap their pets in blankets preparing to leave. She carried her chickens into the house when the coop was underwater. The *Post* reported: "The water mounted. The police boat came and, finally, with tears in her eyes, she allowed herself to be rowed ashore with her husband."

Not all of the news was grim. Lawyer Arthur Wadleigh dropped a fishing line into his basement and caught a 15-inch pickerel. In Uxbridge flood waters washed away soil revealing a safe that was stolen in Boston the month before. A photograph was published of a Chicopee husband and wife with a placid Brown Swiss cow watching the flood go by from a second-floor balcony.

The flood caused controversy too. Several issues—familiar to modern readers—boiled to the surface. Complaints about red tape in trying to get assistance made the rounds. Charges of "wholesale chiseling by pseudo flood refugees" were made by the Red Cross. Looters were alleged to be everywhere, and where martial law was declared, tragic confusion surfaced about who was really in charge. Sent by civilian authorities to a Springfield school to inoculate refugees against typhoid, a prominent local doctor was clubbed in the head with a rifle butt by a National Guard private. The doctor suffered five fractures in his skull because he didn't halt and lacked the proper pass.

By March 23, the rivers were receding and the problem moved south to Hartford. After the threat to life in Massachusetts had passed, authorities counted the toll. During the flood twenty-four people had died and more than 75,000 homeless refugees had found shelter in schools, armories, town halls, or the homes of relatives or friends. More than 150,000 people were displaced at the height of the flood. Damage estimates topped $60 million.

For survivors and volunteers, mud, slime, and wreckage waited to be cleared. Farmers surveyed acres of decimated fields where their major crops of tobacco and onions could no longer be planted. Engineers checked the integrity of the bridges and dams that remained standing. Power plants were restarted. Plans were made for replacement and reconstruction, and there was talk of developing a workable flood control plan.

For many victims, though, only memories remained.
Memories of homes they had lost. Memories of the sound of
the raging flood in the darkness, a sound the *Boston Post* said
was "akin to a jungle roar." Memories of river ice flashing by at
unthinkable speeds. Memories of cattle bellowing throughout
a sleepless night as hundreds of trapped animals drowned in
the sudden flood.

CHAPTER 14

RECORD-BREAKING STORM

The New England Hurricane
1938

Late September was the end of the season for many of the summer residents of Cape Cod. Alice Maurer planned to spend one last weekend at the home of her parents on the Falmouth shore before returning to her winter home in Rochester, New York. Alice, her two sisters, and three brothers had enjoyed the family retreat as children. After a serious automobile accident affected her health, Alice left her job as a nurse and had been coming to Falmouth with her parents for the last fourteen years.

The end of the season meant last-minute errands. A car was in town for repairs, and there was always a little shopping to do. Early in the afternoon on Wednesday, September 21, 1938, Alice and her nephew, Henry Maurer III, left for Falmouth, picked up the car from the garage, and visited one or two stores before heading home. "The car might need some gas," Henry mentioned. Alice replied, "It's a short drive. We should have enough to get home." *Besides,* she thought to herself, *I'd really like to get home as soon as I can.*

Henry drove along the shore road with Alice as a passenger. The car ran out of gas between the shore and Oyster Pond. They waited for a while until Gunnar Peterson happened along. Henry accepted a ride back into town to get some gas. "Why don't you come along with us?" Peterson asked. "No, I'll just wait here," said Alice, who planned just to sit in the car and watch the pounding surf.

Near Wareham, on the opposite side of Buzzards Bay, Mrs. Bernice Fitzgerald of Dorchester and her two children, Thomas and Barbara, arrived at her sister's cottage at about 2 P.M. on that same day. "The wind had been bad on the way to the Cape," Bernice remembered. "At times it seemed to be rocking the car . . . but we didn't pay much attention."

Her sister arrived at about 4 P.M. and mentioned that storm warnings were up all over the coast, but there was sisterly talk to catch up on, so they went about their business. When the lights went out, the women just kept preparing their supper by the glow of an oil lamp.

In an age of weather satellites, radar, and instant communications, it is difficult to imagine a time when a hurricane could strike without any real warning, but that's exactly what happened to New England in 1938. In those days storm systems were tracked by piecing together barometric readings in many locations. Charting such information told forecasters that a center of low pressure was heading north along the coast, but their charts told them little about the intensity of the storm. Besides, everyone knew that hurricanes went out to sea and never passed through New England. The United States

Weather Bureau had been keeping records since 1871, and it hadn't happened yet.

Fishermen on the Massachusetts coast knew they were in for a pretty good blow. Experienced boaters knew how to handle a gale. But just hours before the disaster, virtually no one entertained thoughts that the storm of the century was coming.

While the tropical hurricane bolted from the Carolinas up the East Coast, a center of high pressure moved over Nova Scotia. The usual path of northeast storms was blocked. The hurricane of 1938 had only one place to go. Turning left out of the Atlantic Ocean, the unnamed storm crossed over western Long Island and curled north over Long Island Sound. The hurricane's eye was taking a track parallel to the Connecticut River Valley, but a few miles to the west.

We know that a hurricane's circulation delivers the hardest punch to a coastline in the northeast quadrant of the storm. The path of the 1938 storm placed its northeast quadrant, with its screaming southeast winds, directly over a section of the Massachusetts coast that faced the southeast. The unexpected storm also timed its arrival to correspond with high tide. For the stretch of coastline from Narraganset Bay to the head of Buzzards Bay, the combination meant a near total destruction that shattered the record books.

The Weather Bureau reported an official five-minute sustained wind speed at a somewhat sheltered location in Boston at 73 miles per hour—not all that impressive, but well above the previous mark of 56 miles per hour set in 1877. One-minute wind speeds in Boston, though, hit 100 miles per hour, and Harvard's observatory atop Blue Hill registered a phenomenal gust of 186 miles per hour.

The wind speed at other elevations is anybody's guess. E. B.
Rideout went to check the anemometer in his weather station
on top a building in downtown Boston. "I went up to the roof
and I couldn't find any sign of it," Rideout said. "It must have
landed over there on Boston Common somewhere, or maybe
Beacon Hill. If anyone finds it, I hope they will bring it back."

Boston was hard hit. Tens of thousands of trees were
uprooted and felled throughout the metropolitan area.
According to the *Boston Post*, "By the time the anger of the
wind and water had somewhat abated," the Boston Public
Garden "presented the appearance of a jungle." The Arnold
Arboretum suffered "inestimable damage." Falling trees and
bricks killed several people in greater Boston. Shattered plate-
glass windows showered the streets. More than 200,000
homes lost electrical power.

At the height of the storm, two of the four crew members
of the tugboat *Mildred Olsen* drowned when it capsized in
Boston Harbor. Capt. Frank Hopkins and Jacob Theresen
were the lucky ones who were thrown into the water. The captain was quickly picked up by a boat and taken ashore. As
Theresen struggled to swim to a breakwater, Floyd Roland and
his son Rosse tried to pull him into their dory. Wind and wave
soon capsized the rescue boat and all three men then floun-
dered toward the breakwater's hazardous rocks. Michael
Cusano, a soldier from an army base nearby, ran onto the
breakwater and helped pull Theresen out of the water. Cusano
then departed while six other soldiers saw the predicament of
the drenched men and ran the length of the breakwater to
save them. But the storm was increasing in its fury and now
nine men were trapped on the breakwater by the rising wind
and waves.

Hurricane damage at Siegle's Department Store, 1431 Washington Street, Boston. The building was condemned two days after the hurricane hit.
COURTESY OF THE BOSTONIAN SOCIETY/OLD STATE HOUSE: BOSTON STREETS PHOTOGRAPH COLLECTION

A police boat under the command of Capt. Lawrence Dunn then entered the fray. The *Boston Post* completed the story:

> At the risk of their lives the six members of the police boat got close enough to the breakwater to take off the nine men. They used ropes to get the men on the boat. Several times it appeared that the police boat would be dashed on the breakwater and crushed, bringing instant death to all onboard. So precarious was the plight of the police boat that the fireboat *Mathew J. Boyle* was ordered to lend assistance. The craft made the safety of the harbor police station.

On the coastline of Buzzards Bay, shrieking winds also took their toll, but lack of notice and a "tidal wave" were the area's real killers. The *Falmouth Enterprise* reported that "the first intimation to people along Main Street, Falmouth, that the storm was becoming dangerous was at 4 P.M. when a large limb parted from a tree . . . and crashed to the ground." At the same hour Robert Neal, a station agent at a steamship wharf, put two and two together. The tide was as high as he had ever seen it, yet high tide was not expected for another three hours. He started clearing out the station.

For many residents along the shore of Buzzards Bay it was already too late.

Eleanor Brooks went down to a Falmouth beach with a few other sightseers to watch the crashing surf.

> The sea had begun to sweep across the road. A huge sea broke through the [bathing] pavilion sweeping water deeper between ourselves and the higher section of the road. We jumped hurriedly and found the water well above our knees. . . . Someone remarked that two cars were stalled near the bath house . . . We hoped the people had left them in time and suddenly realized there *was* a figure, moving slowly, pulling itself along the strong fence with its cement posts and steel cables, that bordered the beach road.

Eleanor Brooks was watching Alice Maurer.

One sightseer ran for a telephone. Eleanor Brooks sent another car back to the fire station. "We could see the figure by the fence, not moving one way or the other. The surf was drawing nearer. We watched helpless."

While the bathing pavilion broke into splinters, two boys drove up in a car. One stripped off his shoes, rolled up his pants, and was promptly pummeled by surf, but as Brooks observed: "In the thick spume and high surf near the fence we could no longer be certain there was either fence or figure where we first saw someone."

The boy exhausted himself in a second attempt to rescue the strange figure until firemen arrived. They roped themselves together and waded through breakers into water up to their shoulders, but there was nothing they could do. When Gunnar Petersen and Henry Maurer returned with gas for their automobile, the car was in Oyster Pond. Alice was not to be found.

Mr. and Mrs. Andrew Jones built the fourth house on Silver Beach. When the surf broke into their yard at 6 P.M., Andrew tried to start his car, but it wouldn't go. The couple retreated inside. When water entered the house, they retreated to the second floor. When the tide continued to rise, they climbed onto the roof. "When Mr. and Mrs. Fritz Lindskog saw the Jones roof sweeping past their building," the *Falmouth Enterprise* reported, they "tried to tie blankets together to throw as a life line to the elderly occupants. But the wind swept away their frail attempt." The Joneses rode their roof until it crashed and splintered in the surging surf.

Bernice Fitzgerald was lucky enough to survive a long ordeal. While she and her sister prepared dinner by oil lamp, one of them happened to look outside. Surf was pounding over the seawall, and the only road off the seaside island was awash with ocean water. By the time they threw a few things together to make their escape, the sea had already won, the road to the mainland was washed out, and they were stranded.

Bernice and her family were not alone. Twenty-two other residents of the beachfront community were marooned on the small island and almost without shelter. They watched as their cars washed out to sea. Bernice's sister's cottage had just collapsed and "every building on the island was either inundated or destroyed." Every building but one. On a small rise in the center of the island was a two-story cottage. Twenty-two people, mostly from Bridgewater and Middleboro, rushed for their last hope, broke out a window, and entered the small cottage.

Dusk had arrived, the tide was still rising, and every other structure on the island had disappeared or lay in shambles. Bernice told the *Boston Post:*

> We had only been in this place a short time when the water began to lap at the stairs, then came up level with the porch. We decided then to go upstairs. We had to go upstairs, all 22 of us. . . . There were no lights of any kind. We found crackers and tonic. There was no other food.

During the flood Bernice tiptoed partway down the stairs. Furniture was floating in the living room. Water reached the top of the fireplace. But the tide turned at about 7 P.M. and the water receded slowly, saving those sheltered in the cabin. By 11 P.M. rescue crews from the mainland were able to wade onto the island.

News reports blamed a tidal wave for the havoc in Buzzards Bay. Today, we would be more likely to call it a storm surge that hit the upper Cape at about the same time as high tide. Observers watched pleasure boats tossed high onto the shore and estimated that the rogue tide ran as high as 15 feet. In the village of Buzzards Bay, the tide was measured at 12½ feet higher than it had ever been since records were kept. In Somerset a giant oil tanker was pushed upriver from its mooring and deposited on a garage owned by one of the town selectmen.

Reports from towns around Buzzards Bay were shocking. Of the one hundred cottages at Horseneck Beach, none remained. At Crescent Beach in Fairhaven, 5 summer homes survived out of 178. In Wareham 316 houses and cottages washed away or were crushed to kindling in the surf. Thirty-three people died in the areas bordering the Cape Cod Canal. Fifteen people died in Falmouth and Woods Hole, fifty-seven around Fall River.

Many more would have died but for the courage of dozens of unsung heroes. Up and down the stricken coast, volunteers put out in rowboats, skiffs, and dories to rescue their friends and neighbors. The *Falmouth Enterprise* reported that James McInnis and Ware Cattell "stopped at house after house and took boatload after boatload to safety. . . . Soon after dark the two rescuers had to be rescued. Their rowboat was flung against a pole by a treacherous turn of current and they were thrown into the water." Luckily, both men washed up against a tree that they were able to climb to safety.

Similar stories were common in the coastal zone. Three of the dead in Woods Hole were coastguardsmen who were washed into the harbor by a rogue wave while they were working to save other boaters.

No portion of Massachusetts escaped the record storm. "A belt of fallen trees, 50 miles wide and 42 miles long . . . from Athol to the Connecticut border" was reported by the *Boston Post*. Floods and evacuations came to towns and cities in the Merrimack River Valley. On the first day of autumn, orchards throughout the state lost most of their apple crops.

For people in the Connecticut River Valley, it was deja vu all over again. For the third time in eleven years, residents fled their homes in Northampton, Hatfield, Hadley, Springfield, Holyoke, and Chicopee. The waters rose, the lights failed, and 3,000 members of the National Guard were called out across the state.

One day after the storm, the *Boston Globe* summed up the disaster:

> In the work of reconstruction, clearing the debris of thousands of trees, wrecked homes, fallen wires, washed-out roadbeds and tracks, thousands were engaged today. The W.P.A. in Massachusetts suspended all projects . . . to throw 80,000 workers into the breach and speed the cleanup. Transportation and communication facilities were at a standstill. Bridges are gone, rivers have climbed their banks to create inland flood conditions as menacing as the great flood of 1936. And along the sea, where a tidal wave of typhoon proportions smashed its way 1,000 feet inland . . . the shores are strewn with dead bodies.

At least one writer for the *Boston Post* took a different angle. "Old-timers resent the storm bitterly," he wrote. Last week old-timers "squelched all comparative conversations by referring to the winter of '88." Now, the merest child "can match that conversation by citing the hurricane of '38."

CHAPTER 15

TWELVE MINUTES OF HELL

The Cocoanut Grove Fire

1942

November 28, 1942: It was Saturday night in Boston and time for serious celebrations. As usual the weekend meant wedding parties and receptions. During the war years homecoming furloughs or a last night before shipping out also put servicemen, girlfriends, and families in the mood for a good party. On this particular late autumn day, the clash between Boston College and Holy Cross, two national gridiron powers, added to Boston's merry mood. So what if the local team got clobbered in the big game? Saturday night was a time to party.

At the edge of the theater district, in the heart of downtown, the Cocoanut Grove nightclub boasted a national reputation as a place for good times. Since the days of Prohibition, customers, young and old, had flocked to the Cocoanut Grove. Eighteen years later, it was swanky and sophisticated, but very mainstream—a place where everyday folks could rub shoulders with some whose reputations were a bit naughty.

Charles "King" Solomon was the original owner of the Grove, the city's first nightclub. Variously described as a gambler, racketeer, and gangster, Solomon ran the club until he was murdered in another nightspot nearby. By 1942, under the direction of Barnet Welansky, Solomon's lawyer, the Cocoanut Grove had expanded into two buildings. The sprawling establishment sported a dance floor and stage in the main dining room below a balcony where the big shots sat, the huge Caricature Bar off the entry hall, and the popular Melody Lounge in a dark and noisy basement. A new cocktail lounge had been open just ten days earlier. The whole place was decorated with a jungle theme. Palm trees in the dining room and Melody Lounge almost seemed real under the billowing blue of satin skies.

John O'Neil met Claudia Nadeau at a defense plant in Cambridge where both of the young people worked. Nature took its course. On that Saturday in November, John wore his blue suit and Claudia a wine-colored frock with aquamarine trim when they were married at the Notre Dame Church in North Cambridge at 7 P.M. Outside the church, Claudia kissed her guests good-bye. "But just for tonight," the bride said. "This is war and tomorrow you'll all come to my house. We are having a one-night honeymoon."

The bride and groom were taking John's sister, Anna, the maid of honor, and John Doyle, the best man, to the Cocoanut Grove. None of them had been there before, but, as reported by the *Boston Post*, "Claudia and John had decided that for once in their lives, on their wedding night, they would celebrate in fashionable style."

"Dinner at 8 and at 10, we shall have our last toast and we shall leave," Claudia told her sisters.

The four Fitzgerald brothers from Wilmington had a different reason to celebrate. Private First Class Henry Fitzgerald was home on furlough from Hendricks Field in Sebring, Florida. After Thanksgiving dinner with their mother and sisters, Henry and his older brothers, Wilfred, James, and John, got tickets for Saturday's big football game. Along with their dates, the four bachelors then headed off to the Cocoanut Grove for some dinner and dancing to cap a festive weekend.

Joyce Spector and her fiancé, Justin Morgan, went to the Cocoanut Grove on the spur of the moment. Justin was going to enlist in the army the next day, so the couple was spending a last quiet evening together, playing cards and talking until 8:30. "It had cleared off so nice after the rain and he said 'Let's get a breath of fresh air and have a dance.' So we took a cab and went over to the Melody Lounge, just for a Coke and a dance," Joyce told the *Boston Globe*.

As usual the Saturday night crowd at the Cocoanut Grove far exceeded the seating capacity of the sprawling space, even before the theater crowds arrived later in the evening. All the tables in the main room were filled with patrons, and customers congregated in happy confusion four and five deep around the multiple bars.

In a dark corner of the Melody Lounge, amidst the palm fronds, faux rattan, and zebra-striped settees, the light from a small bulb inside a fake cocoanut shell was too much for one of the customers. He unscrewed the bulb.

Stanley Tomaszewski was a good employee. Within two weeks of starting his job as a bus boy, he was promoted to bar boy—serving drinks in the Melody Lounge for $2.47 a night. No one seemed to care that he was only sixteen. On Saturday night he reported to John Bradley, the head barman, that it was too dark to see in the far corner because someone put a light out. "I told him to go over to the corner and turn it on," Bradley later told reporters. "The boy went over and hollered, and I told him to tell whoever put the light off to put it back on."

Getting no help from the customers, Stanley decided to take care of the problem himself. But it was so dark in that corner of the Melody Lounge that Stanley couldn't see to replace the bulb. He got on a chair and struck a match to locate the bulb. He screwed the bulb back in and the light came on. He shook the match out and stepped down onto the floor. He noticed nothing wrong.

The next instant, a few minutes after 10 P.M., sealed the fate of almost five hundred people. Barman John Bradley testified at an inquest convened by the Fire Commissioner, as reported by the *Boston Herald:*

> All of a sudden, someone yelled "Fire!" . . . I jumped out from behind the bar. The palm tree was ablaze, the one in the corner where the light had been out. Then a flash came. I don't know from where. I ran over and pulled the palm tree down and I tried to beat it out. I tried but I couldn't. I yelled for water and threw water on. But it was too late, too far gone. The whole ceiling was blazing. People were hollering and panicky. Oh my God, they were panicky.

Flames engulfed the ersatz palms and flew across the thin cloth that created the lounge's "sky." Mirrors cracked from the heat before customers could leave their seats. "It was beyond human comprehension that a fire should gain such headway in such a short time," a fire expert later stated. Choking black smoke instantly billowed through the room as patrons bolted for the only exit they knew—the stairway out of the basement that led to the club's main entry hall.

While recovering from third-degree burns, twenty-five-year-old Thomas Sheehan Jr., a lucky survivor of the Melody Lounge, remembered that he was so far from the exit door that he saw no hope of escaping up the stairs. He told the *Boston Herald:*

[O]ne big black cloud of smoke . . . came down from the ceiling so that you could not see who was next to you. It didn't stay dark long. The walls were burning. . . . There was no use trying to push through [the crowd of people at the exit] so I stood in the middle of the room as far from the walls as possible, but the heat was terrible. I could feel the skin on my face blistering. . . . There was a pile of people four or five deep at the door, wriggling and shouting on the floor. I ran and dove right over the pile and landed on my head.

Employees of the club knew there was another exit from the Melody Lounge. The barman tried to get some of the screaming customers to exit through the kitchen, but they were in too much of a panic to listen. Bradley did help two coat-check girls, a few kitchen employees, and as many as twenty other people get out through a kitchen door before finally saving himself by diving through a window over the kitchen's service bar.

The stairway that promised escape from the Melody Lounge became a chimney for poisonous smoke and half-burned gasses. As patrons clambered up the stairs and into the club's entry vestibule, heat and toxic fumes chased them all the way. At the top of the stairs, an emergency exit door with a panic bar was locked and welded shut. Desperate customers turned right in the entry hall and scrambled to the main entrance—a revolving glass door. The crush of people trying to push through both sides of the revolving door caused the door to jam, and the bodies piled up.

William Ladd, a *Boston Post* reporter, was a guest that night.

It seemed everybody wanted to be the first to get out. Men and women in their panic began tearing clothes from the bodies of each other. Then they got to that small door on Piedmont Street [the main entrance] and one of the women went down. Then the other men and women fell on top of her and the bodies then just seemed to keep piling up. The people seemed to be fighting each other on the pile.

While customers died in the Melody Lounge, the good times still rolled in the main dining room. Some customers on the street floor first noticed a puff of black smoke. Others claimed that they saw a screaming woman run past with her hair on fire. Most of those patrons were doomed before they knew what was going on. Like a blow torch, hot gases exploded in the large space, shooting flames through the dining room in only sixty seconds. After the first puff of black smoke was seen on the main floor, it was only five minutes before the Cocoanut Grove was a burned-out shell.

Joyce Spector and Justin Morgan had seen the fire start in the Melody Lounge. Joyce ran upstairs to retrieve her coat and was crossing the dance floor when the crowd of customers bolted for the exit. "Flames were shooting up the stairs where I had just come, and more flames were coming through the floor in front of me."

In the tumult a woman tripped in front of her. Joyce reached out her hand to help the woman up.

> Just then a big man pushed me in the back and knocked me down. . . . It's hard to remember how everything happened. I found I was under a table. Then there were feet all around me, and it was hard to breathe and the flames were licking up through the floor. I just kept crawling and being sort of pushed by feet trampling all around me. I didn't know where I was going. . . . I didn't know there was a little back door . . . whoever it was that pulled me out—threw me across the sidewalk. I landed in the gutter.

Justin wasn't as lucky.

At a side entrance on Broadway, another mass of customers jammed together, struggling to escape as thick black smoke rolled over their heads. Samuel Myers, a cab driver, ran across the street to help and "found a large heavy man with his back to the door barring the way. . . . The man appeared to be wildly excited. He was shouting 'Edith! Edith!' when a sailor with a girl on his arm socked him in the jaw, knocking him down and breaking the glass in the door."

"Suddenly," according to Benjamin Ellis, a pedestrian, "a huge sheet of flame burst out through the entrance, setting fire to clothing, hair, hats, evening dresses, and searing human flesh. Those flames belched out fifteen feet into the street. The screams were dreadful. Those people didn't have a chance."

The cab driver thought no more than a dozen or fifteen people were able to escape from the Broadway entrance before the flash of flames. The super-heated fumes had found oxygen at the exits and exploded into flames. Bodies piled up inside the doors blocking all entry or escape.

Pandemonium broke loose on Boston's streets. Severely scorched people, with much of their clothing burned away began jumping from the club's roof. Victims ran screaming up Piedmont Street, their hair and clothing ablaze. Many died in agony on the sidewalk. Others wandered about screaming for lost friends or merely stumbled senselessly along until a bystander offered a hand.

Firemen who had been called to a vehicle fire were just over a block away when the blaze erupted. Almost immediately, firefighters broke open exit doors, ran in hoses to quell the flames, and began pulling out bodies that were stacked like chord wood inside the exits.

"Bodies and victims so badly burned that they were unable to walk, were laid out in rows," in a garage across the street, reported the *Boston Herald*. Many of the bodies were just blackened trunks with clothing torn or burned away. Faces were charred beyond recognition.

Strangely, though, many of the bodies that were recovered later inside the club were hardly burned at all. Toxic nitrous oxide emitted by burning fabric had felled many victims who apparently died almost immediately without pain. The *Boston Globe* quoted a prominent physician who stated that the poisonous fumes that may have killed as many victims as the flames acted as an anesthetic. "I talked with scores of injured and dying. I was amazed that none of them could remember any sensation of pain from burning," the doctor said.

"Bodies I have examined with my assistants had the appearance of those soldiers gassed in the first World War," a medical examiner told reporters. "People died too quickly to fight for their lives."

Death was random in the Cocoanut Grove. Survivors and victims often sat shoulder to shoulder. Billy Payne, a singer at the club, saved ten patrons by leading them downstairs and into a huge icebox in the basement. A trombone player foiled the grim reaper by ducking into a refrigerator. But a customer who hid in a telephone booth was quickly incinerated.

Only twelve minutes elapsed from the first flicker of flame to the last injury to cause death. A parking attendant across the street heard horrible, shrieking screams coming from the Cocoanut Grove. Suddenly, ten minutes later the screams ominously ceased.

In the midst of the inferno, heroes emerged. Frank Balzarini, the headwaiter of the Cocoanut Grove, was the man who was able to fold back the wings of the revolving door at the main exit to allow patrons to escape. Then, according to the *Boston Herald*, "Forced into the street by the crowd that rushed through the door he had just opened, Balzarini . . . pushed his way through the crowd into the burning building and rescued at least a half dozen unconscious women before he himself was killed."

Hundreds of ordinary citizens responded to the emergency. As many as seventy-eight taxicabs, numerous private vehicles, and one *Boston Globe* delivery truck became instant ambulances ferrying victims to Boston's hospitals. Soldiers, sailors, military police, Boston policemen, cabdrivers, and civilians used overcoats as stretchers to carry the dead and dying away from the grisly scene. Overwhelmed, emergency

The exterior of the Cocoanut Grove nightclub after the deadly fire.
COURTESY OF THE BOSTON PUBLIC LIBRARY, PRINT DEPARTMENT

rooms soon didn't even try to identify victims. They just treated the suffering and did their best.

Fortunately, the arsenal of medical weapons had lately increased. As the *Boston Herald* reported, "The work of emergency Civilian Defense medical services, the American Red Cross, and Boston's hospitals, together with donated blood plasma, sulfa drugs, and burn ointment, [were] credited with saving scores of lives and alleviating suffering."

When blood plasma ran short at the Massachusetts General Hospital, Boston patrolmen Thomas Hussey and Richard

Butler flagged down four city busses. In short order fifty riders volunteered to interrupt their journey to give blood.

After the smoke had cleared and the charred remains were removed, newspapers demanded explanations. Day after day, new revelations appeared on their front pages. Faulty wiring, lax enforcement of fire codes, locked doors, underage employees, fraudulent fireproofing, an unlicensed electrician, lack of permits, and political corruption all floated to the surface for public inspection.

The owner, Barnet Welansky, went to jail. The bar boy, Stanley Tomaszewski, was never charged. An official cause of the fire was never established. The inquest revealed that the city of Boston had few laws to protect patrons of public spaces like the Cocoanut Grove: no regulations on using fire-resistant materials, no regulations requiring exit signs, no regulations prohibiting revolving doors, no regulations requiring sprinkler systems, and no regulations governing decorations. The Cocoanut Grove fire taught the city of Boston some hard lessons.

The hellish night club fire took 492 lives, including those of 51 servicemen. Just over 200 people were able to survive. John O'Neil and Claudia Nadeau had been married less than four hours when they died together in the fire. On the night of November 28, 1942, the widowed mother of Henry, Wilfred, James, and John Fitzgerald lost all four of her sons.

CHAPTER 16

IT COULDN'T HAPPEN HERE

The Worcester Tornado
1953

On June 9, 1953, readers of Worcester's *Evening Gazette* scanned the headlines with mixed emotions. The front-page story about a killer tornado in Michigan and Ohio brought concern and sadness for the storm's victims, but also the comforting thought that the devastation caused by such massive winds could never happen here. Tornadoes, after all, always strike in the cornfields of the Midwest, not in the hills of old New England. Little did those readers know that a murderous twister was preparing to pillage their own hometowns that very afternoon.

Striking at about 5 P.M. on that rainy day in June, the deadliest tornado in New England history tore a 25-mile path through a dozen communities in central Massachusetts. Beginning in the town of Petersham northwest of Worcester, the tornado swept southeast through Beverly, Rutland, and the northern end of the city of Worcester. The funnel cloud then passed into Shrewsbury before splitting into two prongs and disappearing to the south and east. Hitting without warning, the nightmare storm took less than half an hour to blast its swath of destruction.

George Jones and his wife had lived on their Petersham farm for only eight days when they stood in their new home and watched a heavy rainstorm approaching beyond a hill to the northwest. They were the first people to see the killer tornado as it formed its funnel cloud. "When we saw trees drawn up into the funnel, we wasted no time getting into the basement," Mr. Jones said. He grabbed his wife and dashed to the cellar. In just a few moments, the roaring cloud had passed overhead and then all was quiet. The roof of their house was damaged and trees that had stood in their yard since colonial days were uprooted and blown down. Only a concrete pad remained where their barn had once stood.

"It missed us," said Mr. Jones.

"Thank God," his wife replied.

As the swirling storm raged into the next town, other victims would not be so lucky. In Holden mechanic Donald Buxton was greasing a customer's car at the end of a long workday. The big garage doors were closed because of the afternoon's heavy rain. Buxton told the *Springfield Daily News,* "I heard a zinging sound, and the first thing I knew, my garage started to crumble. The car on the lift blew over hitting the customer, and the lift clipped me when it was falling."

Spinning to look toward the street, Buxton then watched in disbelief as his young station attendant, Jon Holmes, was blown clean through the garage. A green car that was parked at the curb flew 25 feet through the air to the entrance of the service bay. "I jumped out of the way and then got hit by cinder blocks. The customer was buried in the blocks. He's in bad shape," Buxton recalled as he nursed his bandaged arm and sore shoulder. Holmes wound up beneath a pile of debris behind the garage. The customer's car was a total loss.

Early June is a time when many college students return home for summer vacation. Ray Sterling, a student at Cornell, was driving with his mother on the Worcester Turnpike in Fayville. When he saw the twister coming, he pulled into a gas station to wait for the storm to pass. Both managed to survive when the car was picked up, turned over three times, and dropped 150 feet from the station.

Peter Volmes was fortunate enough to be only a witness and not a victim. A graduate of Syracuse, Volmes was also driving on the Worcester Turnpike when he saw trees, powerlines, and houses coming down. Blinded by the heavy rain, Volmes got out of his own car and found another vehicle on its roof with both of the occupants dead. He told the United Press: "Twenty yards off the road I saw another car with its roof smashed in. There were three people hurt. They asked me if I had any bandages. I didn't have any, but I gave one man my handkerchief."

In Worcester, commencement exercises were held a week before the storm. The fortunate timing saved countless lives when the twister completely demolished dormitories and administrative buildings on the campus of Assumption College. Two nuns and a priest died. Luckily, no students were there to be injured.

Atomic bombs and nuclear testing were hot topics in 1953, but it was a year that also saw more than its share of violent tornadoes. Politicians were quick to suggest a connection. While the United States Weather Bureau and the Atomic Energy Commission denied that A-bomb tests were to blame for the nasty weather, at least one congressman called for an

Aftermath of the deadliest tornado in New England history.
ASSUMPTION COLLEGE ARCHIVES

investigation. But Dr. Harry Wexler, chief of the Weather Bureau's scientific services division, patiently explained that "the A-bomb is not a weather maker. It doesn't pack enough energy. . . . [A]n afternoon thunder shower is a bigger energy machine than a standard A-bomb." In other words compared with the energy unleashed by the Worcester tornado, an A-bomb is rather puny.

Scientists at the Blue Hills Observatory joined in attributing the New England tornado to a rare set of meteorological circumstances—not to A-bomb tests. Tornadoes are born when air masses that have extremely great differences of temperatures at different levels of the atmosphere collide. Usually, explained the meteorologists, by the time they reach the East Coast and meet hot air from the South, Pacific cold fronts warm up too much to cause twisters in New England. The rare Worcester tornado was spawned by the same unusually sharp squall line running ahead of cold Canadian air that brought tornadoes to Michigan and Ohio twenty-four hours earlier. Typical of large tornadoes, the Worcester storm brought lightning, thunder, rain, and hail. Its awesome funnel cloud screamed with winds swirling somewhere between 300 and 500 miles per hour.

The immense power of the rare New England storm may excuse the local papers for continuing to exploit the A-bomb theme. The *Springfield Daily News* reported that eyewitnesses compared the damage in Worcester with "pictures they had seen of the damage wreaked by the atom bombs on Japan in World War II." In Worcester the *Evening Gazette* carried the news that "six victims of the tornado . . . are being treated for the same type of blast injuries to their lungs as that caused by an atom bomb explosion."

Within the swath of destruction, homes and businesses were pulverized in each of the small towns that stood in the path of the storm. In Fayville Joseph Noberini, a patrolman, was sitting with his family in the front room of their home when he saw wooden planks flying through the air outside. "There was a terrific noise. Things started falling, window glass and shingles all over us. All sorts of things were all over the kitchen." As soon as the storm passed, he desperately dug through the wreckage of the house next door. Beneath the debris he found the bodies of his sister-in-law and nephew.

In Shrewsbury, fire department captain Lawrence Kershaw knew what that twisting black thing was the second he saw it. He told the *Worcester Evening Gazette:*

> [T]he air was filled with flying things, planks, beams, broken chairs, parts of beds. The twister seemed to be picking the buildings it was to destroy. It would dive down and wreck a house and then maybe skip one or two, then come down again for another. It seemed to rise and fall, like waves, picking up a part of a house, chewing it up and then spitting out the pieces.

Damage was severe in rural sections in the storm's path. Dazed cattle lay in a field with stanchions still fastened around their necks. Sixteen-year-old Marshall Lytle ran to a collapsed barn on the Weagle farm. "The cows were mooing all over the place, just sitting there and not moving about much—but there was no roof, no walls, nothing—just the cows, mooing and mooing." The young man also discovered the body of the hired hand beneath the barn's debris. "Blood was all over. His face and chest were covered with blood. I almost fainted."

But the heavily populated city of Worcester was the primary target of the twister's malevolent fury. More than 200,000 souls lived in the city, and many of those residents were concentrated in housing projects and veterans homes in the northern end of town. As fate would have it, this densely populated region received the brunt of the storm.

Before the storm the Brookside Home had the facilities to care for 300 people. After the twister the wreckage was nearly complete. The dormitory barracks, the farm buildings, the laundry, and the garage were all leveled. Joseph Sullivan, age sixty-three, was one of twenty men who were plunged 18 feet into a basement when a stairway gave way. Sullivan told the *Worcester Evening Gazette* that after the roof was blown off, they ran for the stairway, but it had been torn away.

> We all landed in the basement. I was knocked out. When I came to, I looked up. No roof, no walls, nothing left but the foundation. My friends were there with me, all out cold.

In fact five of his friends were dead. The main building lost its roof but was largely spared. Only the fact that most residents were eating dinner in the main hall kept the death toll from climbing higher.

Before the storm 3,000 people lived in the Great Brook Valley public housing projects. While private homes nearby went undamaged, the Curtis Apartments with 300 units and Great Brook Valley Gardens with 600 units suffered direct hits.

For one witness who spoke to the *Worcester Evening Gazette*, the full horror of the twister's devastation didn't seem real until he viewed the remains of the Great Brook Valley veterans housing project.

> It looked like it had been pounded by a heavy artillery barrage. Houses were torn from their foundations and reduced to scrap lumber. Kitchen sinks stood in open lawns. Baby carriages and garden furniture littered the area. Bedding, pots and pans, chairs and tables, and kitchen curtains were all scrambled together like a crazy rummage sale.

In the aftermath of the corkscrew storm, the National Guard sealed off the area of the housing projects, while rescue teams chopped down locked doors and probed through mangled debris in a desperate search for the missing. Ken Mallet left his dry cleaning shop as soon as the wind died down and hurried to the scene of the devastation. His delivery truck soon became a makeshift ambulance. He told the *Worcester Evening Gazette:*

> I made four trips altogether. There was one load with a boy, eight or ten, and he died on the way. There was another one. A girl about six, with her left leg hanging by a thread. Nearly everybody was bleeding. I had 'em packed in like sardines.

When night fell, the only lights in the neighborhood were either cast by emergency floodlights or flickered from handheld flashlights as crews continued to probe the wreckage.

In all the mayhem caused by the killer twister, the fate of the Oslund baby gripped the public's attention and came to symbolize the tragic event. Alone at home with her two-week-old son, young Mrs. Oslund snatched the baby from its crib and ran outside when the twister approached. "I thought it would be safer outside," the devastated mother wept. Recovering in the Holden Hospital from her own internal injuries, Mrs. Oslund said "the wind tore the baby from my arms and carried it away. Then I was knocked down and I don't remember anything else."

For three days local papers reported the futile efforts to find the Oslund baby. The mother had been found lying in the road more than 60 yards from her home, so a frantic and intensive search had to scour the entire neighborhood where 160 homes had been demolished. As many as 150 friends, neighbors, and concerned citizens tore through tangled debris for two days.

"Where can we look now, what can we do?" a weary searcher asked. "We're searching as much as we can and everywhere we can. There aren't many more places we can look." Finally, on the third day Melvin Gardephe, a neighbor and friend of the Oslund family, put an end to the awful ordeal. He spotted the child's body beneath the rubble of several houses more than 400 yards from the Oslund's home.

As usual everyday heroes emerged in the wake of the disaster. In Worcester seventeen-year-old Richard Paretti pulled a pair of twin boys from beneath the wreckage of a three-story tenement building. Throughout the region, police, firemen, volunteers, and military personnel poked and prodded through acres of debris to release and treat scores of trapped victims.

Lighter moments were few and far between. An unidentified woman hurried into the Red Cross emergency response unit and asked to be allowed back into her home. She wanted to look for her false teeth that the twister had blown out of her mouth. Karl Walz Jr. was completing his paper route when the twister hit. He had nothing to do but cling to a tree. A friendly neighbor called him into her home just before the tree was uprooted by the wind and swept away. In Worcester a frantic mother called the police looking for her child. She was told that her one-year-old had been found safely wandering along a sidewalk several blocks away.

The terrible winds of that June afternoon killed thousands of songbirds by stripping many of them of their feathers. The winds carried a copy of a Worcester newspaper 40 miles to

Boston. After the storm dropped baseball-sized hail on parts of central Massachusetts, it picked up birth certificates, checkbooks, photographs, and a music box and deposited them as far away as Quincy.

The Worcester tornado left ninety people dead and as many as 10,000 people homeless. Many of the surviving victims were simply left wondering in stunned disbelief what had hit them. In thirty minutes, without warning, a storm that couldn't happen here had changed their lives forever.

THE GREATEST RESCUE IN MARITIME HISTORY

The Sinking of the *Andrea Doria*
1956

On the warm summer night of July 25, 1956, the *Andrea Doria,* sleek luxury liner and pride of the Italian Line, skimmed through calm Atlantic waters in heavy fog just 43 miles off Nantucket Island. Among the passengers who embarked in Genoa, Naples, Cannes, or Gibraltar were titans of industry, Hollywood personalities, foreign correspondents, and well-known political figures. Also onboard were immigrant families with young children hoping to start a new life in America and elderly naturalized citizens returning from a visit to the "old country" perhaps for the last time.

As the clocks passed 11 P.M., about half the passengers were enjoying the "last night" party in the ballroom after more than a week at sea. The rest had retired to their cabins in anticipation of an early arrival in New York City the next morning.

Ruth Roman, the Boston-raised movie star, was dancing in the ballroom at 11:20 P.M. as the orchestra played "Arrivaderci

Roma." Her three-and-a-half-year-old son, Richard Hall, was sleeping below decks attended by his nurse in cabin 82.

In cabins 52 and 54 on the upper deck, the Cianfarra family had just turned in. It had been a good trip for the family, with two wins at bingo and a $95 prize in the ship's pool. Camille Cianfarra, Madrid correspondent for the *New York Times,* and his wife, Jane, already slept soundly in their bunks. In the connecting cabin Linda Morgan, age fourteen, pulled on her yellow pajamas and climbed into the berth nearest the porthole. Her stepsister, Joan Cianfarra, age eight, curled up in white pajamas. The girls whispered together before eventually turning off the light and drifting off to sleep.

Alfred Green invited his new friends Col. Walter Carlin, a New York political figure, and Carlin's wife to join him for a farewell drink late that evening, but the Carlins were feeling tired. They excused themselves and returned to cabin 46; while Mrs. Carlin retired, Walter Carlin began to brush his teeth in the small bathroom at the far end of their cabin.

Back in the ballroom young Martin Sejda, age fifteen, got bored with the adult party and slipped outside for a walk on the deck. As described by the *Boston Herald:*

> He found himself in a sightless world. Thick veils of fog mantled the ship, blotting out the sea and sky. [Martin] could barely make out the outline of the rail just across the deck. As he felt his way toward it, the ship's whistle roared sounding a hoarse-voiced fog warning.

The *Andrea Doria* was following "track C" on her approach to New York, a route that brought her close to the Nantucket Shoals Lightship in an area known as "the Crossroads of the

Atlantic." Ships sailing to and from Europe or traveling between eastern ports in the United States or Canada generally passed through the area. The narrow shipping channel was often congested and the home of frequent fog.

While the *Andrea Doria* sped west through the crossroads at close to 22 knots, nearly top speed, the *Stockholm* of the Swedish American Line sailed east through the crossroads nearly 20 miles north of its expected course. The smaller Swedish liner had just departed New York bound for its home waters, where it might need its steel reinforced bow to sail through floating ice.

The *Andrea Doria* sailed with 1,134 passengers and a crew of 572. The *Stockholm* carried 534 with a crew of 200. Both ships were equipped with modern radar. Why the collision occurred was a puzzle immediately after the crash. Even today, the disaster seems improbable. One ship was traveling too fast for the foggy conditions and the other was off its appropriate course. Still, why weren't they able to avoid each other?

Each ship had "seen" the other on radar fully a half an hour before the collision. In simple terms each captain interpreted his charts and radar information in directly opposite ways. One thought the ships would pass each other on the port (left) side. One thought the ships would pass each other on the starboard (right) side. At the last moment, thinking they were avoiding a collision, the *Stockholm* aimed directly at the *Andrea Doria,* and the *Andrea Doria* turned broadside to the other ship. Ultimately, the shipping lines settled their differences and accepted shared responsibility for the disaster.

Martin Sejda thought he saw a glimmer of light out there in the foggy darkness, but he knew he was mistaken. He turned to rejoin his parents when something shocking appeared. What he saw was the *Stockholm*'s lights just seconds before the crash. In the ballroom several dancers also spotted a blaze of light through the portholes, just before the staggering crash. It was 11:22 P.M.

The sharply angled bow of the *Stockholm* tore into the starboard flank of the *Andrea Doria* just behind the bridge. With three shivering thrusts, the bow of the Swedish liner tore 30 feet into the bowels of the larger ship in a shrieking howl of scraping and tearing metal. When the *Stockholm* retreated, the gash in the *Andrea Doria*'s side formed the shape of an upside down pyramid, fully 40 feet wide at the top and narrowing to a point below the water level.

The cabins occupied by the Cianfarras suffered a direct hit. Cabin 52, where Linda Morgan and Joan Cianfarra slept, was obliterated. It simply ceased to exist. In cabin 54 Camille Cianfarra was pushed through a mangled wall of metal studs into cabin 56, where he lay fatally injured. His wife, Jane, was also thrown into the adjoining room, where she found herself with a broken leg pinned in the wreckage. Near her Martha Peterson, an occupant of cabin 56, also lay pinned against the bulkhead with two broken legs and a broken back. Dr. Thure Peterson, Martha's husband, was the luckiest of the bunch. The bow of the *Stockholm* somehow pushed him through a gap in the twisting walls into cabin 58, where he lay unconscious.

(On the Friday after the collision, headlines in the *New York Times* reported the tragic loss of their correspondent Camille Cianfarra and his two daughters, Linda and Joan. Edward P. Morgan was the natural father of Linda Morgan and a newsman for ABC radio in New York. That night, he broadcast the whole heart-wrenching story of the tragedy that befell the Cianfarra family but never mentioned his personal connection.)

The sudden impact of the collision staggered Walter Carlin in cabin 46. Stunned, he managed to regain his feet and felt his way to the area where his wife slept. As reported by the *New York Times,* "He saw nothing but a gaping hole. The side of the ship had been sheered off and Mrs. Carlin had vanished . . . a victim of the tragedy."

The "unsinkable" *Andrea Doria*—as the *Boston Herald* would have it—featured eleven watertight compartments that extended up to "A" deck, about half way up the hull. The *Stockholm* had only ruptured two of those compartments. But the gaping hole on the starboard side caused the *Andrea Doria* to tilt or "list" almost immediately as ocean water poured into the massive gash. Quickly, the decks of the stricken liner canted to twenty-five degrees, and the starboard edge of "A" deck dipped beneath the surface. Massive amounts of seawater poured into the ship above the watertight compartments The *Andrea Doria* was doomed.

Ruth Roman hurried back to her cabins (82 and 84). Smoke filled the hallways. She quickly awoke her young son and told him that they were going on a picnic.

In cabin 80 Richardson Dilworth, the mayor of Philadelphia, was thrown out of his bed. He and his wife later told the *New York Times* that they "had to crawl down the passageway and up the gangways because the boat had tilted so badly. It must have taken us twenty minutes to climb up to the boat deck."

Bad news awaited on the open decks. No announcements from the bridge instructed passengers what to do or told them of the ship's condition. Seawater and oil splashed on the tilting decks. Dilworth told reporters later that "the decks were like skating rinks. Half the passengers were over 45. . . . Quite a few people got broken arms on the slippery decks." Without being told, most passengers soon discovered that they were better off without their shoes.

But even worse news soon troubled the endangered passengers and crew of the *Andrea Doria*. A major design flaw created a classic catch-22. The ship would stay afloat with a list of less than twenty degrees, but the lifeboats would not deploy with a list over fifteen degrees. When lifeboats were really needed, they didn't work. The doomed vessel was already listing more than twenty-five degrees and would eventually reach a list of forty degrees or more. Because of the severe list, the lifeboats on the port side swung inboard and hung over the deck. They would not slide into the water. The eight lifeboats on the starboard side hung out over the water far away from the deck. The starboard boats would have to be launched without passengers. The injured and elderly would then have to climb down the side of the tilting hull to get to the rescue boats.

As the night wore on, passengers began to congregate in groups on the high (port) side waiting for rescue with scant information and little assistance. Inside the sinking ship Dr. Thure Peterson began a frantic struggle.

When he came to, Dr. Peterson fought his way back to what was left of his own cabin. He found his suffering wife pinned against the bulkhead. When he couldn't free her from the heavy steel, he gave her a shot of morphine and went off to look for help. Back he came through the smoke and confusion with Giovanni Rovelli, a ship's waiter. Now two men struggled to release Martha Peterson, but still it was no use. "Meanwhile," according to the *Boston Herald,* "he heard Mrs. Cianfarra's cries for help." Again, the two men failed in an attempted rescue, this time of Mrs. Cianfarra, but another trip through the tilting decks produced a pair of wire cutters that freed Mrs. Cianfarra from the bed springs that gripped her broken leg. Once more Dr. Peterson turned his attention to his wife. With time running against them, Dr. Peterson and Rovelli located an automobile jack to lift the beams that held Martha. They hauled the jack through the sinking ship and struggled to put it in place. But now it was too late. Martha Peterson was dead.

A collision at the crossroads of the Atlantic meant, at least, that help would not be far away. The freighter *Cape Ann* was the first rescue ship on the scene, but the small freighter carried only two lifeboats. Even as seamen began shuttling back and forth between the freighter and the sinking ship, it was clear that many more lifeboats were needed.

The *Ile de France*, the sleek star of the French Line, had departed New York City just thirty minutes before the *Stockholm* and was already due east of Nantucket Island. When replacement captain Raoul de Beaudean heard the distress call from the *Andrea Doria* at 11:35 P.M., he acted without hesitation. He knew it would push the tight schedule of his transatlantic greyhound back at least thirty-six hours, but he also knew his duty as a seaman. "Despite the fog I raced at 22 knots and reached the *Andrea Doria*'s position south of Nantucket [at 2 A.M.]."

In the darkest hours of that awful night, the stage was now set for what the *Boston Daily Globe* called "the greatest mass rescue in maritime history." For the *Boston Herald* it signaled "a brilliant new chapter in the saga of seafaring."

The *Ile de France* lay 500 yards off the stricken ship and put ten lifeboats in the water. The crew of the *Andrea Doria* strung

ropes and netting over the side. As one male passenger
remembered it: "We formed chains of hands on the [tilting]
deck and passed the women down the chains until a member
of the crew picked them up and helped them over the side and
down the ladder."

According to the *Boston Daily Globe:*

> Elderly passengers clambered down the ropes, chil-
> dren were tossed through the air and caught in spread
> blankets, injured were slung over in cargo nets. The
> entire transfer was carried out in the fog and darkness
> lit only by searchlights from the ring of rescue ships, in
> just two hours and 36 minutes.

As the fog lifted lifeboat crews risked their own lives as
they shuttled back and forth between the sinking liner and the
rescue ships. As the *New York Times* noted, the rescue crews
"faced continuing perils through the hours before dawn. . . .
While the huge Italian liner kept listing a frightening forty
degrees to starboard, the rescuers braved the possibility that
their own boats would be drawn under the dark Atlantic if the
vessel heeled further."

During the rescue women and children were evacuated
first, and lifeboats ferried their passengers to different rescue
vessels. As a result many families were separated, and authorities remained confused about how many people were still
missing or had already been saved. For families and relatives
the anxieties would last for days until after all of the rescue
ships had returned to safe harbor.

After amusing her son with a balloon during the hectic
wait to get off the ship, Ruth Roman climbed over the rail with

her child in her arms. As they neared a lifeboat, a seaman tied the child to his back and carried him down to a waiting boat. Edging her way down to the water level, the actress was horrified to see the boat that held her child pulling away without her. Even though she was confident that her son was safe, Ms. Roman still endured a long, grim vigil, as did relatives of other survivors, until the rescue ship that held her son finally returned to port.

There was confusion on the *Stockholm* too. The crew's quarters on the Swedish ship were located in the bow, where several sailors died in their sleep at the first moment of impact. The heavily damaged ship was able to stay afloat and would later limp back to New York. In the meantime a seaman named Garcia was assessing the damage to the *Stockholm*, searching a once-graceful bow that was now smashed into a blunt tangle of steel. Suddenly, he heard the cries of a young woman. There in the twisted wreckage, he found a dazed teenage girl, smeared with blood and with a badly broken arm. But this made no sense. The girl's name simply did not appear on the list of passengers on the *Stockholm*. Slowly, Garcia and the girl realized what had happened. Beyond all logic, the girl in the bow was a passenger from the *Andrea Doria*.

Linda Morgan was alive! Miraculously, when the *Stockholm's* bow took dead aim at the Cianfarra's cabins, it had scooped up the fourteen-year-old and carried her out of the sinking ship. As the *Boston Herald* described it: "The nose of the Swedish ship . . . literally plucked a sleeping child from her berth and bore her back to safety upon a cushion of crumpled steel." Linda had no idea what had happened. Later, she told reporters that she thought she was still on the *Andrea Doria*. All she knew was that she woke up, started to scream, and that

The last seconds of the ocean liner Andrea Doria *going down after colliding with the ocean liner* Stockholm *off Nantucket.*
LIBRARY OF CONGRESS, PRINTS & PHOTOGRAPHS DIVISION, PHOTO BY HARRY A. TRASK, LC-USZ62-64156

a man (from Cádiz) looked down at her. She thought she probably had been lying there for some time.

By dawn the fog had lifted, seas were calm, and a beautiful day was in the offing. At 4:58 A.M. the *Ile de France* started her engines and signaled a message to the world: "All passengers rescued." With no other fanfare the French ship raced back to New York with more than 700 survivors.

Of course, deaths occurred on that summer night. A four-year-old Italian girl died from head injuries after her desperate parents tried to save her by tossing her into a lifeboat. The last fatality was a middle-aged man who suffered a heart attack onboard a rescue ship on the way back to port. Five crewmen were killed in the bow of the *Stockholm* and forty-six passengers succumbed on the *Andrea Doria*. But after a massive collision of two crowded ships, the safe return of nearly 2,400 people was a historical achievement.

In less than twelve hours and just 2 miles from the spot of the crash, the pride of the Italian Line saw daylight for the last time. The *New York Times* described her final moments:

> Geysers created by tremendous pressures sent white cascades into the bright sun to make living jeweled columns that vanished almost as fast as they rose. The vessel's powerful propellers, or screws, were high in the air, jutting from the stern. It was nine minutes after 10 under brilliant summer sky, when the *Andrea Doria*, in a final plunge, went down in 225 feet of water, her hull glistening, her shroud a rain of spray caused by her violent death.

SIXTEEN-STORY RESCUE

Building Collapse in Brighton

1971

In the tumultuous days of January 1971, Vietnam and Cambodia were the focus of the world's attention as headlines reported deadly attacks and ominous hints of a wider war in Southeast Asia. Closer to home, politicians expressed confidence in efforts to halt inflation while front pages throughout the nation blared the news of the conviction of Charles Manson and three young women in the grisly Tate-LaBianca murders in California.

On Monday morning, January 26, Robert Delaney ignored the newspaper headlines and went to work as he had for thirty years. That day, the husky fifty-seven-year-old construction worker left his home in Cambridge to report to a job site in Brighton. On the same day Paul Scopa Jr., age nineteen, grabbed a chance to earn a few dollars during a recess from college. Son of the foreman on the site, Scopa reported for his first day of work on the same job as Delaney. In all, about 150 laborers and tradesmen were employed at the construction site at 2000 Commonwealth Avenue, not far from Chestnut Hill Reservoir and overlooking Boston College.

Monday was only one day shy of "top out" day on the sixteen-story concrete structure. Final pours of concrete on the roof would complete exterior construction of the $5 million luxury condominium. Inside the shell of the building, workers swarmed over countless unfinished tasks. Al Fiorilli, a carpenter, reported to work on the fifteenth floor. Daniel Tintindo, forty-four, a welder, and James Cingolani, twenty-six, his helper, were in the basement working on the sprinkler system. Ciraco DiIorio, forty, a laborer, was tending to his job in the stairwell on the sixth floor.

The project was progressing nicely and the work had become routine, until 3:22 P.M., Monday. While workmen were pouring concrete on the top floor, without warning, a portion of the roof collapsed. "At first the top floor corner just fell onto the next floor, and you could hear the creaking and groaning," the young foreman's son, Paul Scopa Jr., remembered.

Directly beneath the trouble on the fifteenth floor, Al Fiorilli saw the ceiling buckle, "Then a carpenter ran down yelling get the hell out of here. I took off down the back stairs and other guys were running down ahead of me and behind me."

"Workmen were waving people away. Concrete and wood started to fall and the corner of the roof started to give way," said a local resident who was passing by.

Robert Delaney had been operating his crane, ferrying material and supplies to workmen on various floors of the building when he was shocked by a terrible sight. As he told the *Boston Globe:*

I was operating a power hoist putting materials up the building. I looked up at one point and saw a compressor on the roof plunge to the ground and go through a masonry shack. I jumped out of my cab and ran over to the shack thinking the mason might have been inside. He wasn't.

At that instant, however, Delaney began to understand the danger that thirty or more workmen faced on the roof when he saw the top section of the building beginning to sway back and forth.

As the seconds rushed by, near panic struck the area. Police sirens wailed and fire trucks raced to the scene. In the middle of the chaos, not thinking about the danger, Delaney sent his power hoist aloft and carefully positioned his bucket to rescue workmen trapped on the shivering roof.

I sent the hoist aloft and picked off twenty or thirty men. I made two trips, probably three, but I can't remember exactly. There was a shower of everything from the top, rocks, bricks, mortar, and it was obvious a section of the roof was collapsing. The only thing I could do then was sit there and pray for the men above, and pray they got out alright somehow.

Delaney had rescued thirty men, but heroic efforts had only just begun that day. Young Scopa estimated that about ten minutes passed between the time a portion of the roof collapsed and when the side of the building came down. They were a fateful ten minutes. Michael Papasedro, twenty-nine, a foreman on the job, went back into the two-story basement garage to look for Tintindo and Cingolani, the welders who were part of his crew. It was the last time Papasedro was seen. DiIorio came down to the second floor, and then for unknown reasons, he returned to the sixth floor, perhaps to retrieve his tools. He was never seen alive again.

An eyewitness reported that an unidentified man "appeared on the sixth floor of the structure yelling 'Help me, help me, help me, can anybody hear me?'"

> He was yelling for maybe four or five minutes and I yelled back. Any number of people in the crowd heard him and saw him. But we were all being pushed back by the police and I didn't see anybody go to help him.

Just before all the supports of the balcony gave out, a pair of workmen hurried up to the cab of Delaney's crane. It was William Murphy and Frank DiSimone, two men that Delaney had already saved with his hoist when he lowered them from the roof of the trembling building. Murphy and DiSimone knew that several men were still trapped high on top of the building. One was Patrick McNulty, who was working on the roof when the cave-in began. All of them, McNulty later explained, were trapped because they were afraid to move for fear of stimulating the further collapse of the structure.

Shedding concern for their own life and limb, the two workmen who had already cheated disaster told Delaney about the men on top and asked for another lift. Delaney himself described the event to the *Boston Herald Traveler* with characteristic modesty:

Billy Murphy, who lives in Quincy, and Frank DiSimone from Derry, N.H. way came up and made me hoist them upstairs. I did it. . . . I hoisted them all the way to the top where they could see the men who were up there. . . . Murphy and DiSimone spotted three men trapped on the other side [of the roof collapse]. They yelled to me to guide them over in the bucket. I did and the men got into the bucket and came down safely.

Unfortunately, Delancy would pay a price for his courage.

The whole top of the building was swaying by then and debris was falling all over the place. The minute the men in the bucket reached the ground they ran to avoid the falling mortar and bricks and rubble. I ran too. Then something struck me and knocked me to my knees.

Just thirteen minutes after the first portion of the roof collapsed, massive sections of the concrete building simply let go. James Adams, a graduate student who happened by, watched as the three men were saved in the concrete bucket, and described it this way:

Then we heard a crackling, like glass breaking, and a piece of wood fell from the top. Then the whole thing started cracking and crumbling and it collapsed from the top right down to the ground, making a sound like breaking dead branches off a tree.

Reinforced concrete weighs 150 pounds per cubic foot. From both sides of the building, 30-foot-long concrete slabs that were built as balconies tore away and fell like dominoes. With a grumbling roar slabs weighing up to twenty tons ripped open exterior walls in their grinding plummet to the ground. As reported in the *Boston Globe,* "8 and possibly as many as 12 of the 16 floors of reinforced concrete dropped almost exactly vertically and landed one upon another in the basement like playing cards stacked in a deck."

The *Boston Herald Traveler* reported that "several score workmen and firefighters barely escaped being buried alive between the collapse of the section of the roof, and the collapse that brought all the balconies to the ground." As 4,000 tons of debris hit the ground, according to the *Globe,* "the collapse shook the ground for blocks around and sent huge chunks of debris flying out onto busy Commonwealth Avenue." Immense clouds of dust billowed up from the pile of rubble.

Hazardous shards of construction debris were flung up to 100 yards across a major thoroughfare and onto the tracks of the MBTA. Trains were halted, traffic was jammed, and additional police and rescue units found it hard to get to the scene. Throngs of curious spectators assembled around the skeletal ruin. Eventually, police cordoned off the area and evacuated several hundred residents who lived in nearby apartment buildings.

Uncertainty took over. Did everyone get out? Were all accounted for? Could anyone be alive in that mass of rubble? Ominously, a truck driven by two workmen sat abandoned at the site. As darkness fell, officials realized that four men were missing: Ciraco DiIorio, Michael Papasedro, James Cingolani, and Daniel Tintindo were officially announced as being trapped in the ruins.

Construction workers returned to the scene to help with the rescue effort, but the deadly building had not finished taking its toll. As the *Globe* reported, any rescue attempt "was made doubly dangerous by tons of concrete hanging from the sides of the building, held only by twisted steel reinforcing rods."

Floodlights were brought to the scene to help the rescue effort, but rescue couldn't begin. "The building is still snapping and popping inside and I don't know if more might fall," said George H. Paul, the deputy fire chief. "I couldn't possibly send men into the building until I know it's safe."

At St. Elizabeth's Hospital that evening, Delaney was treated for a broken left wrist. Miraculously, he was one of only three men slightly injured in the massive collapse. As he was hugged by his wife and two daughters, Delaney continued to deflect attention away from himself, crediting Murphy and DiSimone for their heroism, before his wife made it clear that he was not going back to the site to help dig the missing men out.

Often in rescue missions many quiet heroes receive no recognition. After a thirty-six-hour delay, day-and-night rescue efforts began at the Brighton site. A crane too large for Boston's tunnels was disassembled and transported to the scene. But brave men still had to scramble over rubble in the shadow of deadly hanging debris or cut steel with torches as they hung suspended from a 280-foot crane. Utility services to the building had already been disconnected, but rescue officials remained concerned because several tanks of propane gas were buried under the wreckage. The risk of explosion was high as heroic workmen hacked the rubble into smaller pieces and used acetylene torches to cut through a maze of reinforcing rods.

Two days after the disaster, Richard Duane, supervisor of a crane crew remained optimistic that some of the men might survive in air spaces created by the rubble, but the fire chief gave them no chance.

Amidst growing frustration and offers of help, the work went tediously on. The area around the collapsed building was too small to fit more than two cranes. As hours turned into days, hope began to evaporate, except for that of the anguished families of the victims. Boston's building commissioner estimated that crews were able to remove ten tons of debris per hour. Rescue could take as much as two more weeks.

In time the urgency of the rescue waned, but crews continued to work around the clock. After three days rescuers were able to lift the concrete lid from a 20-by-30-foot section of basement garage. They found more concrete, but no sign of the missing men.

Spectators dwindled as the raw days of January stolidly drew to an end. A rumor circulated that authorities had found a workman's shoe but were keeping the information quiet. On the Sunday after the collapse, nearly one hundred families that had been evacuated from nearby buildings were allowed to return to their homes.

Finally, on February 1, rescuers made their first grim discovery. After six days of continuous digging, and seven days after the collapse, a body was discovered 15 feet down in the 25 feet of rubble that filled the upper basement. After five more hours of digging by hand with picks and shovels, the body was removed. Crushed, mangled, and pierced by steel rods, the body was identified by its personal effects as Ciraco DiIorio, age forty, husband and father of four.

Even as the hopeless task of retrieval dragged on, a commission began an investigation into the cause of the collapse. On days and nights when loved ones took medication and couldn't sleep, cranes continued to move concrete, and experts speculated about how concrete can be weakened if it is poured when it's too cold.

By mid-February, after nearly three weeks, even the relatives of the missing knew that all hope had vanished. The collapse of the luxury condominiums at 2000 Commonwealth Avenue had left four widows and eleven fatherless children. But for the efforts of men named Delaney, Murphy, and DiSimone, the loss would have been much higher.

CHAPTER 19

SLOW-MOTION DISASTER

The Sinking of the *Argo Merchant*

1976

In the early-morning hours of December 15, 1976, the captain and crew of the *Argo Merchant* had no idea where they were. The 648-foot Liberian tanker had departed Venezuela bound for Salem, Massachusetts, carrying 7.6 million gallons of number 6 oil. The crew knew they were sailing up the East Coast, but the last time they knew their exact position was two days earlier off Cape Hatteras, North Carolina.

Somewhere out there, Capt. Georgios Papadopoulos reasoned, they should be able to spot the Nantucket Lightship southeast of Nantucket Island. After that, setting the course would be easy: Head north in the shipping lane east of the Nantucket light, then curl around Cape Cod and straight into Salem Harbor.

What he had to avoid, the captain knew, was the area west of the lightship, the hazardous Nantucket Shoals. A vast region of swirling currents and shifting sand stretching south from Nantucket Island, the shoals were a graveyard for large ships.

With a draft of 30 feet, his low-riding tanker full of oil would have little chance in that patch of open sea where ship-killing sandbars lurked less than three fathoms (18 feet) beneath the surface.

At 1 A.M. Captain Papadopoulos came to the bridge to check the navigation charts. From there the crew should be seeing a beacon from the critical light, but all they saw was the dark of the winter night. The *Argo Merchant* was equipped with a gyrocompass, a magnetic compass, a radio directional finder (RDF), and radar, but not with long-range navigation (LORAN). The officers had plotted their course by the old-fashioned method of dead reckoning, drawing their progress on a chart as confirmed by sightings of the sun and stars.

The men in the chart room faced a number of basic problems. The gyrocompass had been giving erratic readings. The "true north" reading on the gyrocompass disagreed much more than usual with the shifting "magnetic north" readings given by the ship's magnetic compass. Also, the dead-reckoning course they had plotted didn't account for drift caused by the winds and tides. Even though the course they plotted seemed to steer them directly into the shoals west of the lightship, the captain relied on charts that predicted that the wind and tides would push the ship to the east and out of danger.

Nerves were taut by 4 A.M. As the helmsman recalled, everyone was moving up and down the bridge looking out. Three senior officers, the captain; George Ypsilantis, the chief mate; and George Dedrinos, the second mate, were on the bridge trying to find the lightship. By their calculations they should have spotted its beacon more than an hour earlier. Were they that far off course or had headwinds and a heavy load just drastically slowed them down?

The captain saw lights off the port bow, but radar confirmed that he was looking at fishing boats. The chief mate turned on the RDF, searching for the radio signal that would also locate the lightship. He had no luck with the finicky unit, but the depth finder told them that the ship was still in deep water.

By 5:30 A.M., nothing was making sense. The radio signal from the Nantucket Lightship was good for 100 miles. With visibility at 7 miles, they certainly should have found the gleam of the lightship's beacon well before now. The radar still showed nothing, so Ypsilantis tried again with the RDF. Thank God! He got a signal. He did a quick calculation. Nantucket Lightship was dead ahead. They weren't really off course. They were just behind schedule.

But still they saw no light, and the depth finder gave a reading of 20 fathoms.

Ypsilantis was still concerned. Instead of waiting for dawn, he used a sextant to take sightings of Polaris (the North Star) and Arcturus, another bright morning star. His ancient method of navigation placed the *Argo Merchant* miles to the southeast of the Nantucket Lightship. Great! The RDF, the dead-reckoning course, and the star sites all put the tanker in different positions. The depth finder cast doubt on the sextant readings. The lack of visual contact with the lightship cast doubt on the RDF. The captain went with his intuition. He cast his lot with the position determined by dead reckoning.

Winds and tides can change off Nantucket from month to month. The *Argo Merchant* only carried a chart for November that was several years old. The captain didn't have a modern chart for December telling him that prevailing tides would push his ship into the shoals. He ignored a depth-finder reading that placed his bulging tanker in less than 90 feet of water. He didn't know that his chief mate had performed a miscalculation with the RDF. The plodding ship had long since passed to the west of the Nantucket Lightship and was about to die in the shoals.

The bottom of the *Argo Merchant* ground into the hard sand of Fishing Rip on Nantucket Shoals 27 miles southeast of Nantucket Island a little before 6 A.M. The aging tanker was 24 miles west of her intended course, due north of the Nantucket Lightship.

Twice Captain Papadopoulos ordered all engines full astern. For thirteen minutes the ship's propellers churned up silt and sand from the ocean bottom in a desperate attempt to free the tanker from the shoals. But the ship just shivered in place. "The ship did not move," the captain stated in a deposition. "When we felt every endeavor was impossible, we notified the Coast Guard at 7 A.M."

From midships back to a point close to the stern, the rusting hull of the *Argo Merchant* had come to rest on a thick finger of hard sand only 18 feet beneath sea level. The bow projected out over shallow water, while the stern hung over a trench that had a depth of 54 feet. Many miles from land, wind and waves rolled and lifted the creaking tanker. With each passing hour the *Argo Merchant* was slowly pounded further into the sand.

The *Boston Globe* greeted the news of the grounding with a definite yawn. Just another ship caught on the shoals. Because no injuries or oil spill was reported, the incident rated a few short paragraphs on page 3, just above a story about a dead battery in Cleveland.

Reporters from Fall River, Cape Cod, and the islands had a better grasp of the implications of the ship's predicament.

Millions of gallons of gooey oil were stuck on a shallow sand-
bar just 27 miles southeast of the shell-fishing beds and pris-
tine beaches of Nantucket Island. The same gooey cargo was
less than 50 miles northwest of the tip of Georges Bank, one of
the most productive fishing grounds in the world.

The scallop beds in Madaket Harbor would be in the path of
any spill. Madaket accounted for 40 percent of the shell-fishing
industry on Nantucket, and creatures from lobsters, to scallops,
clams, gray seals, and humpback whales would be threatened
by a spill. Nantucket's financially critical tourist trade would
also be imperiled. "It's damned ironic that whale oil built this
island, and crude oil may destroy it," said Arnold Small, execu-
tive secretary of the Nantucket Board of Selectman.

On Cape Cod a fishing industry spokesperson put the
grounding in perspective. "Fishing Rip is Chatham's backyard.
The Chatham fishermen feel very personal about this. All of
them at one time or another have wet a handline in that rip."

At Georges Bank the consequences would be worse.
According to reports in the *Cape Cod Times*, the fertile fishing
grounds due east of Massachusetts contained 20 percent of the
world's ocean harvest and accounted for a $75 million annual
catch for New England fishermen. Stocks of cod, flounder, had-
dock, hake, halibut, and catfish could all be devastated in a
major spill.

When the Mayday message was received from the stranded
tanker, the Coast Guard stood ready to respond. The *Argo
Merchant* had a history of mechanical problems and minor
spills. The ship was due to be inspected before it entered Salem
Harbor. Now, with news of the grounding, the U.S. Coast
Guard's Atlantic Strike Team swung into action. Based in
North Carolina, the Coast Guard team was designed to respond

quickly to oil spills. Within the hour helicopters took to the air. Men, equipment, and ships were headed for Nantucket Shoals.

A Coast Guard cutter and four helicopters were on the scene by 8:30 A.M. and offered to take the thirty-eight–man crew off the grounded ship. Captain Papadopoulos declined. Other than some water in the engine room, the tanker didn't seem to be in immediate danger. Four pumps were lowered from helicopters to drain the engine room. If the ship could be lightened, maybe tugs could drag it off the bar.

But the job of saving the tanker was going to be truly daunting. And it all depended on the weather. For starters all the rescue equipment in the immediate area was designed to save much smaller fishing boats. The pumps that first reached the tanker would barely hold their own pumping 15 feet of water out of an engine room that was 30 feet high. The pumps would be rendered useless if they sucked in the tanker's oil. Number 6 oil is as thick as caramel, toothpaste, or peanut butter. Special heating units on the tanker kept the oil as warm as 120 degrees so the gooey mess could be loaded and unloaded. It would take a minor miracle to salvage this sticky sludge without a spill many miles from shore in the middle of 12-foot seas.

In the first hours after the grounding, calls went out for special equipment: two ocean-going tugs with barges big enough to hold seven million gallons of oil, fenders big enough to keep barges and tugs from striking the tanker's hull, deep-water moorings to keep the barges in place, heating units to warm the sluggish cargo, high-capacity pumps to drain water and oil, and Skycrane helicopters to deliver the heavy goods. It was going to take days to gather the equipment needed. It could take weeks to pump out enough oil to pull the tanker out of the sand. The

During rescue operations a U.S. Coast Guard helicopter hovers over the 648-foot Liberian tanker Argo Merchant *that ran aground on the shoals of Nantucket with a cargo of 7.6 million gallons of heavy crude oil.*
LIBRARY OF CONGRESS, PRINTS & PHOTOGRAPHS DIVISION, LC-USZ62-83424

strike force would probably need more time than Nantucket's fickle weather was likely to provide.

While equipment was on the way, damage-control teams from the Coast Guard cutters *Sherman* and *Vigilant* moved onto the stricken tanker. Plan A was to stabilize the ship to keep it from breaking up. Plan B was to lighten the ship and drag it off the bar. Plan C was to pump out as much oil as possible before it spilled into the sea. The small pumps were rigged and started, and by 2 P.M. most of the tanker's crew was taken off the ship. So far, only light oil from the engine room had contaminated the ocean. The cargo was still intact.

By the time the strike team leader, Lt. Cdr. Barry Chambers was choppered out to the scene, night had fallen and a small sheen of oil drifted out from the hull. Ominous buckling was beginning to show in the steel of the tanker's deck. Water was again rising higher in the engine room, and all the power on the ship was off.

Chambers was a no-nonsense guy, experienced in oil spills. He understood the size of the task that lay ahead. His public statements tried to be accurate but optimistic. He told reporters that it was going to be rough.

Pilots risked their lives to land a 400-pound "Adapts" high-capacity pump on the tossing deck of the tanker after dark. Chambers and his strike team dragged the massive pump to the engine room and reversed the rising tide, but their joy was short lived. "We could look up and see, 20 feet above our heads, how the bulkheads were stretching and bulging as we were getting the water level down," Chambers said. "Oil was oozing out along the rivets as the straining bulkhead was stretching the rivets."

At 9 P.M., just fifteen hours after the grounding, the flood in the engine room of the *Argo Merchant* was again uncontrolled, and the weather was getting worse. A spokesperson for the Coast Guard informed the press that the ship was taking on water in the rough seas.

By 1 A.M. the next morning, a ten-degree starboard list put that side of the ship underwater, the stern was 18 feet lower than the midsection of the ship, and the rest of the crew and strike team had been evacuated in the middle of the night.

Weather forecasts predicted winds increasing to 45 knots and 15-foot seas. The handwriting was on the wall.

By Friday, the second day after the grounding, the Coast Guard had to admit that "some of the oil was lost in the rough seas last night. It's spillage from the top of the cargo tanks . . . not from the hull or anything like that." Each wave that washed over the tanker lifted the hull slightly and set it down again. In effect the ocean had devised its own pumping system, one that sprayed number 6 oil out of the vents of each of the ship's thirty storage tanks. The spokesperson was wrong on one point. Oil was draining from the tanker's hull. One and a half million gallons were already lost. The oil slick covered a curved slice of ocean 65 miles long.

Still, the strike team wouldn't quit. There were still six million gallons of oil to keep off Nantucket's beaches and away from the fragile fishing grounds of Georges Bank.

With the decks slick with oil and swept by ocean waves, the strike team risked life and limb going back onboard the *Argo Merchant*. Maybe there was still time to off-load the rest of the oil. They secured hatches and plugged leaking vents. On Sunday a Skycrane helicopter delivered two Yokahama fenders that were tied to the side of the oil-soaked listing ship—each fender weighed over two tons. With the aid of a tug, the crew also dropped one of the tanker's huge anchors well away from the bow to try to stabilize the hull. They placed four mooring buoys for off-loading barges, to stabilize them while oil was being off-loaded.

But wind and wave are determined enemies. On Tuesday at 9 A.M., the worst news arrived at the Coast Guard command center on Cape Cod. The bow of the *Argo Merchant* had "jackknifed" and broken off. Not completely separated from the rest of the ship, the bow section swung on a hinge of plate-metal hull and pointed back toward the sinking stern. The *Cape Cod Times* reported that observed from an airplane gallons of oil could be seen pouring out of the cargo hold.

Within hours the bow broke again and floated free of the rest of the ship. One last time Chambers and men from the strike team were lowered into danger. They landed on the oil-drenched bow that now was listing twenty degrees and pointing into the air at a sixty-degree angle. This time, though, their goal was not to prevent an oil spill but to eliminate a hazard to navigation. The strike team opened the bow's empty tanks and all its hatches to sink the obstruction. Chambers thought of it as climbing an oil-soaked steel mountain.

Already, oil-soaked gulls and seabirds were washing onto Nantucket's beaches. The oil slick from the *Argo Merchant* was 95 miles long and 25 miles wide. Experts disagreed about what would happen. The oil will sink and poison shellfish and the eggs of ocean fish for years, many said. The oil will float and contaminate fish harvest, ruin fishing gear, and kill migrating whales, others claimed. Nobody really knew.

The heavy number 6 oil floated like ice and clumped together in vast patches that were called "pancakes." The lethal mess covered thousands of square miles, but where was it going to go? As December wore on, oceanographers became confident that Nantucket, Martha's Vineyard, and Cape Cod would be spared. Instead, shifting winds and tides gradually pushed the congealed oil toward the southern end of Georges Bank. Fishermen in Fall River predicted the end of their way of life.

At the time the wreck, the *Argo Merchant* was the worst oil spill in U.S. history. A few lessons were learned, but they were lessons that are hard to accept. Coast Guard admiral William Benkert was quoted as saying: "Under the weather conditions in the past week, no matter what the design of that vessel, no matter whether it was properly or improperly equipped, once this grounding occurred, the story would have ended the same way."

According to Kenneth Biglane of the EPA: "I'm afraid there is no known technology to clean up the spill while it is at sea. We have to let it run its course."

In the face of large ocean spills, even valiant efforts often have little effect. When all was said and done, core samples proved that the oil from the *Argo Merchant* did not sink to the sandy bottom. Millions of gallons of oil drifted over the tip of Georges Bank, across the continental shelf, and into the Gulf Stream. Wind and waves broke the spill up until it had completely dissipated. Environmental damage was slight, and disaster was averted. At least in the face of this oil spill, the world learned that it's good to be really lucky.

WIND, WAVES, AND SNOW

The Great Whiteout
1978

Ninety years makes a difference. For almost a century the blizzard of 1888 remained the winter storm that defied comparison. That legendary blizzard of yesteryear crippled western Massachusetts and demonstrated the frailty of the state's newfound reliance on rail and telegraph service. Fast-forward ninety years: Eastern Massachusetts would be hit with a record-breaking storm that challenged our love affair with automobiles and interstate highways for the first time.

In 1978 technology also made a difference. This time we saw the storm coming. "Here We Go Again," said the headline in the *Boston Herald American.* "Brace Yourself!" warned the *Boston Globe.* On February 6, 1978, Monday morning papers carried predictions of 6 inches of snow, with winds gusting up to 40 miles per hour. By the time the evening editions were printed, the havoc had already started. Forecasters revised their estimates up to from 8 to 16 inches of snow. Their predictions weren't even close.

In a quirky sort of way, Mother Nature gave Massachusetts a break in the winter of 1978. A two-day storm in late January had dumped 20 inches of snow on much of the state. Residents were reminded just how miserable driving could be in a big nor'easter and how unpleasant the prospects were of being stranded at their place of work. As soon as the flakes began to fall late in the morning on February 6, commuters started making plans to leave work early to get home.

Still, thousands of commuters didn't leave their jobs early enough. When the storm hit, it hit with a major thud. Flurries began in Boston at 10:20 A.M. Before noon, seven large trucks overturned in one accident on Route 128. By 3:30 P.M. major highway arteries were already blocked. Wind gusts over 60 miles per hour reduced visibility to almost nothing in swirling and drifting snow.

In midafternoon a tractor-trailer jackknifed on the Southeast Expressway. A spokesperson for the Metropolitan District Commission (MDC) knew that in the middle of a blizzard, the otherwise routine event could escalate into a major migraine headache. "Nothing worse could have happened to the MDC than to have a truck jackknifed into both left-hand lanes," Michael Goldman said in exasperation. "Just as the storm hits, this happens."

The storm was just getting started. By 7 P.M. winds were gusting to 79 miles per hour. State police reported that Route 9 was a parking lot. On Route 128, one of the state's most heavily traveled commuter routes, southbound traffic was at a standstill. Northbound traffic was moving at 1 foot a minute. Interstate highways were jammed as far west as Worcester. Thousands of cars on highways in southeastern Massachusetts were stranded in the mounting snow.

The worst highway nightmare occurred in the southbound lanes of Route 128 between Route 9 on the Wellesley-Newton line and the Route 138 interchange in Canton—the area clogged by the tractor-trailer jackknife. As the *Boston Globe* reported, the entire stretch of highway "was blocked by abandoned cars, three and four abreast, covered with snow and bumper to bumper for miles."

John Hill spent a long Monday night in his car and walked a mile to a shelter on Tuesday morning. "I was scared and don't mind admitting it," he later told reporters. "All I could think of was if I fell and injured myself they wouldn't find my body until spring."

John Tarbox, another motorist stranded on 128, told the *Boston Globe* how he was rescued:

> I got stuck here Monday on my way home from work. I stayed until 5 Tuesday morning and then took one of the buses the State Police brought. They took us to St. Bartholemew Church in Needham where there were about 2,000 other people. Some people were panicked out there . . . but most people handled themselves well.

The drivers and passengers in more than 4,000 cars were stuck in the century's worst blizzard. Many huddled in their vehicle overnight. Some slogged through mounting drifts and managed to walk to safety. In time civil defense buses rescued others and carried them to makeshift shelters. The extraordinary conditions called for extraordinary responses. Volunteers in snowmobiles skimmed past stranded vehicles and carried hundreds of motorists off the highways. Many of the cold commuters were welcomed in nearby homes or industrial plants until after the storm lifted. Teenagers on snowmobiles ferried hot drinks out to motorists who wanted to stay with their cars.

After the National Guard was activated, three Huey helicopters from Otis Air Force Base even assisted with multiple rescues.

Mary Codair left her job at a shoe factory mid-Monday afternoon. The bus got stuck on 128. "If anyone had told me last week that this was going to happen I would have told them I wouldn't live through it . . . . I was scared to death," Mrs. Codair told reporters. Unable to leave the bus, she and the driver and three other passengers endured a sleepless night. "I was emotionally upset. I know I was frightened. The driver told us if we had to stay in the bus another night he didn't have enough fuel to keep us warm."

Early Tuesday afternoon, snowmobiles arrived and carried Mrs. Codair and the others back to the shoe factory where she started. Her final adventure was a ride in Huey chopper that lifted her from the factory to a Red Cross shelter at a local school.

The experience was far less stressful for others. Carla Fitzgerald left work, got stalled in traffic for four hours, and ran out of gas after only a quarter mile. She abandoned her car and walked to the Merkel Enterprises plant. "We had all the comforts of home. Being a food processing plant, we ate baked ham, beans, minestrone soup, bacon, bagels and cream cheese, cake, and even had some champagne. What's more, we played cards and I won $11 in a poker game."

In downtown Boston the major storm seventeen days earlier had prepared people for the big blizzard. Most commuters got out of town. The hotels were not jammed, and workers who needed to stay on the job showed up with almost everything they needed. One cheerful telephone worker told a reporter, "I brought everything this time except the martinis—pajamas, slippers, bathrobe, change of clothes, hairspray . . . we know what's ahead and we intend to enjoy it to the fullest."

Hockey fans are always a different breed. The first night of the storm was the first night of the Beanpot Tournament—the annual battle for hockey supremacy among the colleges of Boston. In spite of the howling blizzard, 11,000 fanatic fans turned out at Boston Garden to watch Harvard and Boston University move on to the finals. Somehow, the transit authority kept the "T" running until midway through the second game. Only about 130 die-hard fans were actually stranded. Garden employees broke out free food, an impromptu hockey game went on at the far end of the ice, and those who were really exhausted fell asleep in the locker rooms.

By the time the storm wound down on Wednesday morning, parts of Massachusetts were under 4 feet of snow. Wind gusts as high as 125 miles per hour piled the white stuff into towering drifts, and many urban landscapes looked like white barren deserts. In Boston the storm set three weather records: total snowfall for a single storm (27.5 inches), total snowfall in twenty-four hours (23.6 inches), and total snow on the ground (29.0 inches).

All that was left was the digging out. State highways were closed east of Worcester and stayed closed in Boston for a week. An airlift brought forty military planes full of troops and heavy equipment to Logan Airport to help clear the paralyzed highways. Five hundred and fifty lane-miles of snow and abandoned vehicles had to be cleared from the major routes that fed the city. An estimated 3,000 cars and 100 tractor-trailers were buried on Route 128 alone.

With so many abandoned cars, plows had a hard time maneuvering around and clearing the roads, according to a spokesperson for the Department of Public Works (DPW). A representative of the Army complained that because of the depth of the snow, it was sometimes hard to tell if there even was a car beneath it. As described by the *Boston Globe,* "Clearing the . . . southbound lane [of 128] is a piecemeal operation of shovel a space, tow a car, shovel a space, tow the one next to it, shovel a space."

Eighteen-wheel five-ton wreckers, 25,000-pound front-end loaders, and bulldozers manned by the National Guard, army, and DPW finally attacked the clogged arteries from both directions. Abandoned vehicles were dragged out of the snow and parked in the breakdown lanes. DPW buses brought any owners who hadn't already walked out to the scene to drive their cars away. By Saturday the *Boston Herald American* was able to report that the troops "dug a 16-mile path through the snow on Route 128 yesterday, exhuming nearly 4,000 cars and trucks from what had been a quick-frozen burial ground."

In Boston and its inland suburbs, the blizzard of '78 was sometimes frightening and generally inconvenient. One-third of Boston was blacked out during the storm when a piece of windblown roofing smashed a transformer in South Boston. Most schools and many businesses closed for at least a week. Several people died from heart attacks. For most commuters, though, the blizzard was a bit of an adventure and a good chance to spend a few unscheduled days at home with the ones they loved.

For coastal towns north and south of Boston, the blizzard was an unmitigated disaster. Hurricane winds, high tides, flooding, and horizontal snow devastated towns from Revere to Scituate to Hull. Six feet of water flooded streets in Winthrop. Thousands of homes were evacuated in Revere, Scituate, and Nahant. Seawalls were destroyed by high tides in Rockport and Gloucester.

Parts of Scituate were cut off from the mainland by high water. A five-year-old girl drowned when a fire department boat capsized while trying to rescue residents of Light House Point. "I stood on Haverly Road today and couldn't get my bearings," said a town selectman. "There's ocean where the street used to be and houses are floating in the ocean where there never were any houses before. The destruction is unbelievable."

Thursday's *Boston Globe* described the following scene:

All along Nantasket Avenue, rescue crews, neighbors and firefighters were launching small boats to paddle down streets with water eight to ten feet deep. On most streets only the rooftops of cars were visible. Furniture floated on top of the ice-coated water while people stranded in their homes for more than three days, waved anxiously from second and third story windows at rescuers.

Barbara Smith lived in the Sand Hills section of Scituate. When the water began to rise, she put the cat into a safer part of the house. Her twin brother, Arthur, was with her at the time. "The house began to shake from the water and the wind. We began flicking the lights off and on to signal somebody that we were in terrible trouble." A neighbor, Bruce Webb, came to the rescue but arrived just as a wall of the home buckled from a wave and knocked Barbara unconscious. Bruce and Arthur carried Barbara to Bruce's dump truck and tried to drive to safety. After only a few hundred yards the truck rammed a sand bank that the storm had washed across the road. As the ocean crashed around them, they sat in the truck for three hours until other rescuers arrived.

*Snow made highways look like this parking lot during
the Great Whiteout of 1978.* © 1978 JACK MCCONNELL

One-third of Revere was under as much as 6 feet of water. A man drowned in his basement trying to start a pump. Rescue crews worked for fifty hours straight taking only short naps. Amphibious vehicles called "ducks" evacuated as many as 1,100 residents in town. MDC employees in scuba gear rode through flooded areas on a bulldozer searching for victims in submerged cars. Thankfully there were none to be found.

Jerry Villani was driving a snowplow on Broadsound Avenue in Revere and found himself and his truck underwater in a matter of moments. Jerry managed to avoid being a casualty by climbing up onto the sand pile that was still in the back of the truck. After three hours of sitting on his small island in a whiteout blizzard, Jerry was finally rescued.

Early in the storm the Coast Guard received reports that a Greek oil tanker was taking on water off Salem Harbor. Winds were gusting to 100 knots and seas had built to 30 feet. The 47-foot pilot boat *Can Do* left the dock in the middle of the night to offer assistance to the tanker's crew. The five civilian volunteers on the pilot boat had saved many lives over the years. It was an experienced seafaring crew.

The *Boston Globe* reported that "the sea had smashed the *Can Do*'s radar and radio antenna, blown through the windshield and washed out the electrical system." The last communication from the rescue boat reported "navigational" problems at 3:20 A.M. The bodies of the crew washed ashore in Nahant and Marblehead a few days later. Tragically, the Greek tanker they tried to rescue was never in real danger of sinking.

The most visible loss in downtown Boston occurred at Anthony's Pier 4 restaurant. A former Hudson River cruise ship, the SS *Peter Stuyvesant* sat at the dock at pier 4 where it served as an elegant cocktail lounge, beautifully restored and full of antiques. Resting in a special cradle, the ship was attached to the parking lot with 16-inch steel pipe hammered 60 feet into bedrock and secured with forty-ton concrete blocks. It was no match for the blizzard. The proud ship was torn from its moorings and sank close to the pier.

The following Monday, a week after the storm, Massachusetts was beginning to return to normal. Suburban highways were open again, and Boston braced for an onslaught of commuters who were still not allowed to drive cars. The excitement was just about over. Time to get back to work. More snow was in the forecast.

CHAPTER 21

UNDERGROUND MIRACLE

Collision at Back Bay Station

1990

All his life, Richard Abramson wanted to be a railroad engineer. At age forty-one his dream was finally coming true. His boss called him a "railroad fan" and said he was "fascinated with trains." Even on his days off, Abramson often liked to just hang around the train yard in New Haven where he was based.

As a young man Richard took a job doing electrical work for Amtrak. Over the course of seventeen years, he worked his way up to "hostler" or train-yard engineer, shuffling locomotives from track to track inside the railroad yard. In 1987 Abramson made his way into the engineer apprentice program. He studied in a classroom for a month and then spent a week learning the ropes on a locomotive simulator. He passed a written exam on the physical characteristics of his likely route. Finally, on December 10, 1990, his lifelong ambition was fulfilled. For the first time he took control of Amtrak's Night Owl passenger train, supervised, of course, by an experienced engineer.

December 12, 1990, was Richard Abramson's third day at the controls of the Night Owl as an Amtrak apprentice. Standing behind the newcomer was Willis Copeland, a veteran with twenty-five years on the railroad. Copeland was a railroad history buff. Nicknamed "Smiley," Copeland was considered an effective instructor and was respected by his colleagues. But Copeland, in the words of the *Boston Herald*, had a "bad track record." He had been at the controls of several trains that were involved in mishaps in the New York City area. The commuter rail line serving New York actually banned Copeland from running trains into their area south of New Haven for the rest of his life.

Amtrak's Night Owl made a daily run from Washington, D.C., to Boston. Abramson and Copeland boarded the train in New Haven. Together, they piloted the Night Owl's two diesel locomotives and ten passenger cars on the final leg of a trip that was scheduled to end in South station at about 8:40 A.M. After stopping in Providence, Rhode Island, train 66 (the Night Owl) got a call from the Massachusetts Bay Transit Authority asking for a little help. Abramson and Copeland made an unscheduled stop in South Attleboro to pick up about one hundred extra MBTA passengers. As it traveled north toward Boston, the Night Owl was running late.

Back Bay is an underground station below Dartmouth Street in downtown Boston, the last stop before South station and the end of the Amtrak line. Northbound trains rumble into the city on a long, straight stretch of underground track that passes through Ruggles Street station and then turns sharply to the right as it nears the platform at Back Bay. Trains were allowed to hit 100 miles per hour on the long straight approach, but had to slow down to 30 miles per hour for the turn into Back Bay.

"Pinch it in when you get to Ruggles," Copeland told the apprentice. Abramson nodded his understanding of the railroad lingo telling him to hit the brakes when the platform at the Ruggles Street station came into view. The trainee lightly applied the air brakes just west of Ruggles as he was told and throttled down the engine at milepost 226.5, about a mile before Back Bay station.

Right away, both Abramson and Copeland sensed that something was wrong. Afterward, they both questioned the brakes, but the brakes were working fine. Abramson said the train was going 94 miles per hour as it passed the Ruggles Street station. Investigators and witnesses who worked in the station put the speed at 100 or 110.

Abramson squeezed the brakes again—this time hard. By then it was too late. At the speed the train was traveling, braking should have been started at a railroad landmark known as the Pickle Factory, located almost a mile before the Ruggles station. Data recorders proved that the Night Owl's average speed over its last 1¼ miles was 91.8 miles per hour. It covered that distance in forty-nine seconds.

According to experts, a train going as fast as 60 miles per hour could stay on the tracks on the tight 30 miles per hour curve into the Back Bay station. The Night Owl barreled into the turn at 76 miles per hour.

As the Night Owl screamed into the turn on track 2, an MBTA commuter train from Stoughton was slowly rolling to a stop at the Back Bay platform on track 1. The commuter train carried more than 900 passengers in seven cars that were pushed from the rear by a single locomotive. On December 12, 1990, the commuter train's configuration with a massive engine at the back probably saved countless lives.

Abramson and Copeland felt their engine tilt to the left. After that their memories fail. The Amtrak train jumped the tracks 500 feet from the passenger platform and skidded shrieking on its side into the MBTA engine on track 1.

Passengers on both trains were tossed like rag dolls. The two 120-ton engines of the Night Owl plowed into the MBTA locomotive with such force that the MBTA locomotive was bent into the shape of an "L." The Amtrak engines jackknifed 50 feet into the air smashing through the roof of the station and poking a hole in Dartmouth Street. All three engines came to rest across the tracks. Thousands of feet of track were twisted like so much spaghetti.

Firefighters and emergency medical technicians (EMTs) found nothing but bad news. The high-speed collision had ruptured a fuel tank on one of the engines. Diesel fuel poured out, found its way to the hot engines, and immediately ignited. Flying debris and car parts also severed a standpipe in the station. There was no water to fight the flames. Electric lines were cut. There were no lights or ventilation fans. The careening train engines wiped out support columns that held up the station's roof. Emergency crews had to work with the fear of further collapse. Worst of all, the wreck all but filled the narrow underground station.

The general manager of the MBTA, Thomas Glynn, described the conditions to the *Boston Globe:* "They are in a box that is 75 feet wide, 25 feet high and 400 feet long and dealing with 360 tons of wrecked locomotive."

Boston's emergency medical units flew into action. Hospitals were notified and called in extra personnel. Firefighters and EMTs had been on the scene within minutes, but emergency responders were hampered by black choking smoke that hid victims and filled their lungs. To reach passengers in one part of the station, rescuers had to squeeze through a one foot gap between a locomotive and a concrete wall.

Dazed passengers stumbled upstairs into the waiting room of Back Bay station. Maureen Boyden, a commuter passenger, told the *Boston Globe:*

> I was standing up to get out when all of a sudden there was a loud crash and I flew into the air. It was a scary scene. . . . It was horrifying. Luckily we were able to make it out the door. All I know is that my head really hurts and I think I'm going to throw up.

Evelyn Carmichael was blood soaked, leaning against a column, and awaiting her turn with the paramedics.

> We were waiting to get off. It was just another regular day. But then bang. Everything went dark. The car filled with smoke. People were screaming, crying. They were on top of each other. We didn't know which way was out. It was chaos.

Frank Bolton was in the last passenger car at the rear of the MBTA train.

> It felt like the car was being lifted of the tracks and it was ripped open like an aluminum can. . . . The roof of the train just fell in and I looked up and it looked like the roof of the tunnel. It was amazing. I can't believe I'm still alive.

Here's how the *Boston Globe* portrayed the scene down below on the platform level:

Downstairs, shrouded in acrid smoke, the injured, some drenched in blood, some with broken limbs, were strewn about the darkened tunnel moaning in pain as rescuers struggled to free passengers trapped inside the crumbled commuter train parts of which had been reduced to a tangle of broken steel.

In a scene he described as being like a war zone, John Joyce, a lieutenant with the Boston Fire Department, crawled into the overturned wreck of the burning Amtrak engine and found the stunned engineers. Other responders worked with the "jaws of life" for forty-five minutes to free the men from the debris. The injured crew was lifted out of the engine's cab through a smashed window. Abramson suffered broken vertebra, a broken wrist, and facial trauma. Copeland sustained a broken elbow and was transported to the hospital in critical condition from trauma to his head, spinal cord, and stomach.

Other firefighters wormed their way into the wreckage to free passengers pinned by debris or impaled on shards of steel. Lieutenant Joyce helped free a woman trapped in the wreckage. "She should have been cut in two," said Joyce. "There was steel right through the seat she was on. She had an angel on her shoulder."

Michael Walsh, another fire lieutenant, thought that at least nine people who were impaled or stuck on steel had to be extricated from the wreckage. "You couldn't see four feet in front of you," Walsh told reporters. He also told the *Boston Herald* that "most of the firefighters gave their breathing masks to civilians whose faces were blackened by the diesel soot."

As a result of their unselfishness, at least two MBTA policemen and two Boston EMTs found themselves in intensive care due to smoke inhalation. Three days later, Massachusetts governor Michael Dukakis honored the two MBTA policemen, Sgt. James Mulhern and Officer Willie Brown, who risked their lives to save passengers. Also honored were the Red Cross and Salvation Army for their role in relief efforts, and twelve-year MBTA veteran William McCoy.

According to the *Boston Herald:*

> McCoy . . . pushed past burning train wreckage in the Back Bay Station tunnel, then climbed through the window of a derailed Amtrak car to help a firefighter rescue a female passenger trapped inside the rear of the train. . . . After passing the injured woman . . . through a window, McCoy briefly passed out, then came to and climbed out of the wreckage on his own.

Passengers on both trains who were not seriously injured pitched in on the rescue too. Ronald Cormier picked himself up, grabbed an axe, and smashed a train window. "Then I grabbed this lady—I could barely see her, just her form on the floor—and I brought her back and slid her through the window. This guy just grabbed her over his back and ran with her." A construction worker helped EMT Jamie Orsino carry victims and haul equipment for over an hour—even when he thought his foreman would probably kill him for being late.

A report of the National Transportation Safety Board (NTSB) totaled the damage in the Back Bay crash. "On train

66, 7 crewmembers and 43 passengers were injured; on the MBTA train, 5 crewmembers and 351 passengers were injured. Seven firefighters were also injured. The estimated damage exceeded $12.5 million."

Newspapers had a field day with the inexperience of the trainee engineer. "Rookie on the Rails" screamed the headline in the *Boston Herald*. In the end, though, the NTSB placed the blame squarely on Copeland for his lack of adequate supervision as well as on Amtrak for lack of oversight of its training program.

Workmen cut up the locomotives and damaged cars, loaded them onto eighteen flatbed train cars and hauled them away. A 70-by-30-foot hole had to be dug in Dartmouth Street to repair the subway tunnel. Six days after the wreck, Back Bay station reopened for normal use. Dartmouth Street was closed for weeks.

Recovering in the hospital a few days later, one of the unsung heroes of the crash highlighted the most important fact in the horrid event. Robert Breen, one of the first firemen on the scene, suffered smoke inhalation when he quelled the flames on the Amtrak locomotive. He told the *Boston Globe* his story:

> I was on top, looking into the engine. The whole engine itself was on fire. We wanted to make sure the fire didn't get into the cab. I was running out of air. I gave my mask to a civilian. Finally we knocked the fire down. It took awhile. It seemed like a half hour.
>
> I never saw anything like it. It looked like an earthquake I guess. My first thought was there must be fatalities. There was too much destruction.
>
> We expected the worst. We got a miracle.

BIBLIOGRAPHY

BOSTON HARBOR'S WORST SHIPWRECK
The Sinking of the *Maritana* (1861)

Boston Daily Advertiser. "Disasters. & c.," November 4, 1861, p. 4.
Boston Daily Journal. "A Severe Storm," November 4, 1861, p. 3.
———. "News from the Fleet," November 5, 1861, p. 4.
Boston Evening Transcript. "A Heavy Gale, Shipwrecks and Loss of
   Life," November 4, 1861, p. 1.
Smith, Fitz-Henry, Jr. *Storms and Shipwrecks in Boston Bay and the
   Record of The Life Savers of Hull*, privately printed, Boston 1918.

ONE MAN'S COURAGE
The Wreck of the *Eveline Treat* (1865)

Boston Daily Evening Transcript. "Mariners Relieved from Peril,"
   October 25, 1865, p. 2.
Boston Herald. "Wreck of a Maine Schooner Off Nantucket,"
   October 25, 1865, p. 2.
Boston Post. "Disasters, &c.," October 24, 1865, p. 3.
Nantucket Inquirer and Mirror. "Marine Disaster," October 28, 1865,
   p. 2.
New Bedford Daily Evening Standard. October 23, 1865, p. 3.
Snow, Edward Rowe. *Great Storms and Famous Shipwrecks of the New
   England Coast*. Boston: Yankee Publishing, 1943, p. 225.

THE GREAT REVERE DISASTER
Crash on the Eastern Railroad (1871)

Boston Daily Evening Transcript. "Great Railroad Disaster," August
   28, 1871, p. 2.

———. "The Eastern Railroad Accident," August 29, 1871, p. 2.

Boston Herald. "The Eastern Railroad Horror," August 29, 1871, p. 2.

———. "The Eastern Railroad Horror," August 30, 1871, p. 2.

Boston Post. "Frightful Disaster," August 28, 1871, p. 2.

WHOLESALE RUIN
The Great Boston Fire (1872)

Boston Daily Advertiser. "The Fire," November 11, 1872, p. 1.

———. "The Great Conflagration," November 11, 1872.

———. "After the Fire," November 12, 1872, p. 2.

———. "Rain on the Ruins," November 13, 1872, p. 1.

Boston Evening Transcript. "A Great Calamity," November 11, 1872,
        p. 1.

Describing the Great Fire. Boston and New York: Houghton Mifflin
        Company, 1909.

Harper's Weekly. "The Boston Fire," editorial, November 30, 1872,
        p. 934.

Murdock, Harold. Letters Written by a Gentleman in Boston to His
        Friend in Paris. Boston: Houghton Mifflin, 1909.

THE MILL RIVER FLOOD
Failure of the Williamsburg Dam (1874)

Harper's Weekly. "The Mill River Tragedy," June 6, 1874, p. 470.

Sharpe, Elizabeth M. In the Shadow of the Dam: The Aftermath of the
        Mill River Flood of 1874. New York: Free Press, 2004.

Springfield Daily Republican. "Terrible Disaster," May 18, 1874, pp. 1,
        5, 8.

———. "A Disaster Extra," May 19, 1874, pp. 4, 5.

———. "The Disaster Extra," May 20, 1874, p. 4.

Worcester Aegis and Gazette. "Terrible Calamity," May 23, 1874, p. 3.

Worcester Evening Gazette. "The Flood," May 18, 1874, p. 1.

CALAMITY AT DEVIL'S BRIDGE REEF
The *City of Columbus* Tragedy (1884)

Boston Evening Transcript. "A Savannah Steamer Wrecked," January 19, 1884, p. 2.

———. "The Gay Head Disaster," January 19, 1884, p. 4.

———. "The Gay Head Disaster," January 21, 1884, pp. 2, 3, 8.

Boston Post. "Shipwrecked," January 19, 1884, p. 1.

———. "At Devil's Bridge," January 21, 1884, p. 1.

———. "Ocean's Victims," January 22, 1884, p. 1.

———. "Chart Showing Course of City of Columbus in 'Fatal Course,'" February 2, 1884, p. 4.

———. "Every Inch a Man," February 9, 1884, p. 1.

Nantucket Journal. "A Terrible Calamity," January 24, 1884.

Snow, Edward Rowe. *Great Storms and Famous Shipwrecks of the New England Coast*. Boston: Yankee Publishing, 1943, p. 139ff.

SUBURBAN NIGHTMARE
The Collapse of Bussey Bridge (1887)

Boston Evening Transcript. "Another Railroad Horror," March 14, 1887, p. 1.

———. "The Forest Hills Disaster," March 15, 1887, p. 1.

———. "The Bussey Bridge Disaster," March 16, 1887, p. 1.

Boston Globe. "Over 30 Dead," March 14, 1887, p. 1.

———. "37 Dead," March 15, 1887, p. 1.

Boston Post. "Terrible Disaster," March 15, 1887, pp. 1, 2.

———. "Cause of the Wreck," March 16, 1887, p. 2.

Massachusetts Board of Railroad Commissioners. *Special Report to the Legislature in Relation to the Disaster of Monday, March 14, 1887*. Boston: Wright & Potter Printing Company, 1887.

THE BENCHMARK WINTER STORM
Trapped by a Blizzard (1888)

Cable, Mary. *The Blizzard of '88*. New York: Simon & Schuster,
   1988.
Caplovich, Judd. *Blizzard! The Great Storm of '88*. Vernon, Conn.:
   VeRo Publishing, 1987.
Boston Daily Globe. "Storm Swept," March 12, 1888, p. 1.
———. "Cut Off," March 13, 1888, p. 1.
———. "Digging Out," March 14, 1888, p. 2.
Northampton Daily Herald. "Snow and Blow," March 13, 1888, p. 1.
———. "Storm Notes," March 15, 1888, p. 1.
Springfield Union. "Buried in the Snow," March 13, 1888, p. 1.
———. "Fury of the Storm," March 13, 1888, p. 1.
———. "Looking Brighter," March 14, 1888, p. 1.
———. "Into the Light," March 15, 1888, p. 1.
Werstein, Irving. *The Blizzard of '88*. New York: Crowell, 1960.
Worcester Evening Gazette. "Snow Storm No. 23," March 12, 1888,
   p. 5.
———. "Blockaded," March 13, 1888, p. 2.
———. "The Great Storm," March 14, 1888, p. 2.
———. "The End," March 15, 1888, p. 4.

BIRTH OF THE DEADLIEST KILLER
The Spanish Influenza (1918)

Barry, John M. *The Great Influenza*. New York: Penguin Books, 2004.
Beveridge, W. I. B. *Influenza—The Last Great Plague*. New York:
   Prodist, 1977.
Boston Globe. "Measles in Company at Camp Devens," September
   12, 1918, p. 12.
———. "Two More Deaths in Naval Hospital," September 13, 1918,
   p. 4.

———. "Influenza Found in Several Cities," September 14, 1918, p. 10.

———. "Simply Grippe, Rear Admiral Wood Says," September 14, 1918, p. 2.

———. "McCain Proud of His 12th Division," September 15, 1918, p. 6.

———. "Doctors Declare Grippe Is on Wane," September 20, 1918, p. 5.

———. "Postmaster Murray Dies of Pneumonia," September 22, 1918, p. 1.

———. "Influenza Toll in Boston for Day 87," September 24, 1918, p. 1.

———. "Close Theatres, Movies, Dance Halls and All Other Unnecessary Public Assemblages Until Oct. 6," September 26, 1918, p. 1.

Boston Herald. "Influenza Is Spreading to Boston Suburbs," September 15, 1918, p. 1.

Boston Post. "3000 Have Influenza at Devens," September 17, 1918, p. 9.

———. "Ayer Camp Ordered in Quarantine," September 20, 1918, p. 5.

———. "2300 Made Citizens at Devens," September 21, 1918, p. 4.

———. "Postmaster Is Dead of 'Grip,'" September 22, 1918, p. 1.

———. "Theatres and Schools May Close Doors," September, 25, 1918,

———. "Rushing Doctors to Boston," September 28, 1918, p. 1.

Crosby, Alfred W., Jr. *Epidemic and Peace: 1918.* Westport, Conn.: Greenwood Publishing, 1976.

THE BATTLE OF ORLEANS
U-Boat Attack on Cape Cod (1918)

Barnard, Ruth. *A History of Early Orleans.* Orleans, Mass.: Orleans
    Historical Society, 1975.
Boston Globe. "German Submarine Sinks Three Barges," July 22,
    1918, pp. 1–2.
Boston Post. "Shelled by Submarine Off Coast of Cape," July 22,
    1918, pp. 1–2.
Boston Transcript. "'Duds' Struck U-Boat," July 22, 1918.

A STICKY SITUATION
The Great Molasses Flood (1919)

Boston Evening Transcript. "Explosion Kills Several," January 15,
    1919, p. 1.
Boston Post. "Huge Molasses Tank Explodes in North End," January
    16, 1919.
———. "Trapped in Freight Building," January 16, 1919.

WASHED AWAY
The Failure of the Wheeler Dam (1927)

Berkshire Evening Eagle. "Flood Sweeps Becket," November 4, 1927,
    p. 1.
———. "Scores of Lives Endangered, Homes, Bridges, Autos,
    Garages Swept Away. Great Damage Done by Floods,"
    November 4, 1927, p. 1.
———. "Becket Will Rebuild," November 5, 1927, p. 1.
———. "Wheeler Reservoir Dam Found in Fair Condition,"
    November 5, 1927, p. 4.
———. "Reconstruction Work in Becket Is Being Rushed,"
    November 8, 1927.

———. "Becket Victim Had Broken Neck," November 9, 1927, p. 7.

North Adams Transcript. "Becket Selectmen Appeal for Funds to
    Rebuild Town," November 4, 1927, p. 1.

Springfield Daily News. "Woman Drowns at Becket and 25 Buildings
    Swept Away as Reservoir Breaks," November 4, 1927, p. 1.

———. "Becket Still Paralyzed by Flood's Toll," November 5, 1927,
    p. 1.

WATER OVER THE DAM
The Connecticut River Floods (1936)

Berkshire Evening Eagle. "National Guard Called Out in North
    Berkshire; Sand Holds Water Back," March 18, 1936, p. 1.

———. "Guardsmen and Volunteer Workers Labor Mightily,"
    March 19, 1936, p. 1.

Boston Post. "Menace of High Water Is Passing," March 18, 1936.

———. "Floods Spread Disaster," March 19, 1936, p. 1.

———. "Flood Terror Spreading," March 20, 1936, p. 1.

———. "Whole Streets of Homes Swept Away by Floods," March
    21, 1936, p. 1.

———. "Human Interest Tales of Flood," March 23, 1936

Springfield Daily News. "An Abundant Water Supply Is Indicated,"
    March 10, 1936.

———. "Scores Flee Homes in Northampton," March 13, 1936, p. 1.

———. "Menace of Flood at Northampton Grows," March 14, 1936,
    p. 1.

———. Vernon Dam Goes Out," March 18, 1936, p. 1.

———. "Coastguards, Sailors Sent from Boston to Northampton,"
    March 19, 1936.

RECORD-BREAKING STORM
The New England Hurricane (1938)

Boston Daily Globe. "Hurricane Dead 275," September 22, 1938.

————. "N.E. Hurricane Kills 85," September 22, 1938.

————. "N.E. Faces New Flood Peril," September 23, 1938.

Boston Post. "100 Killed in Wild Hurricane," September 22, 1938.

————. "Death List May Reach 500," September 23, 1938.

Fall River Herald News. "Storm Toll Increases," September, 23, 1938.

————. "New Horrors In Storm's Wake," September 24, 1938.

Falmouth Enterprise. "Death, Damage, Daring in Hurricane," September 23, 1938.

————. "Personal Experiences in Falmouth Hurricane," September 30, 1938, p. 2.

TWELVE MINUTES OF HELL
The Cocoanut Grove Fire (1942)

Benzaquin, Paul. *Holocaust.* New York: Henry Holt, 1959.

Boston Daily Globe. "Police Say Busboy's Match Caused Fire," November 30, 1942.

Boston Herald. "450 Die," November 29, 1942.

————. "Boy's Match Set Blaze," November 30, 1942.

————. "State to Indict Fire Guilty," December 2, 1942.

————. "Deadly Gas That Killed Scores Center of Disaster Probe," December 3, 1942.

Boston Post. "408 Dead, 350 Injured in Fire at Cocoanut Grove," November 29, 1942.

————. "Night Club Death List," November 30, 1942.

————. "No Fire Safety Measures Taken by Cocoanut Grove," December 4, 1942.

Boston Sunday Globe, staff report. "400 Dead In Hub Night Club Fire," with numerous related stories and photographs, November 29, 1942.

IT COULDN'T HAPPEN HERE
The Worcester Tornado (1953)

Springfield Daily News. "82 Die in Worcester Storm," June 10, 1953.

————. "Tornado Loss Is 75 Million: 89 Are Dead," June 11, 1953.

————. "Pictorial Record of Worcester Tornado," June 13, 1953.

Worcester Evening Gazette. "Tornadoes Kill 141 in 2 States," June 9, 1953.

————. "87 Killed, 800 Injured in City's Worst Disaster," June 10, 1953.

————. "Tornado Destruction and Suffering 'Impossible to Describe,'" June 11, 1953.

————. "Roads into Area Closed," June 12, 1953.

THE GREATEST RESCUE IN MARITIME HISTORY
The Sinking of the *Andrea Doria* (1956)

Boston Daily Globe. "Liner Sinks—5 Dead," July 26, 1956.

————. "2 Liners Crash Off Nantucket," July 26, 1956, p. 1.

————. "Last 530 Reach N.Y.," July 27, 1956.

————. "Sea Toll 11 Dead, 23 Missing," July 27, 1956.

Boston Herald. "Liners Crash Off N.E. 1634 in Peril," July 26, 1956, p. 1.

————. "Sea Rescue Greatest in History," July 27, 1956.

————. "Toll 30 Dead, 73 Missing," July 29, 1956, p. 1.

Hoffer, William. *Saved.* New York: Summit Books, 1979.

New York Times. "Andrea Doria and Stockholm Collide," July 26, 1956.

————. "Andrea Doria Survivors Arrive Here," July 27, 1956.

————. "Times Man Killed," July 27, 1956.

————. "Stockholm Docks with 533 Saved; 8 Known Dead," July 28, 1956.

SIXTEEN-STORY RESCUE
Building Collapse in Brighton (1971)

Boston Globe. "16-Story Building Falls in Brighton," January 26, 1971, p. 1.

———. "Hero Says 2 Iron Workers Real Heroes," January 27, 1971.

———. "Loose Steel, Concrete Slow Brighton Search," January 27, 1971.

———. "Hunt Pushed through Frigid Night," January 28, 1971.

———. "Body Found in Debris Identified," February 1, 1971.

———. "City Opens Building-Collapse Probe," February 2, 1971.

———. "No Sign of 4 Who Were Working on Falling Building," February 2, 1971.

Boston Herald. "Boston Building Collapses," January 26, 1971, p. 1.

———. "Saved 30 But 'No Hero,'" January 26, 1971.

———. "Grim Rescue Effort Begins," January 27, 1971.

SLOW-MOTION DISASTER
The Sinking of the *Argo Merchant* (1976)

Boston Globe. "Leaking Tanker Stuck off Nantucket," December 15, 1976, p. 3.

———. "Coast Guard Fears Tanker 'Catastrophe,'" December 18, 1976, p. 1.

———. "New Figures on Spill," December 20, 1976, p. 1.

———. "Argo Merchant Breaks Up," December 22, 1976.

Boston Herald American. "Tanker Aground, Oil Perils Cape," December 16, 1976, p. 1.

———. "Nation's Worst Oil Spill Perils Georges Bank as Tanker Splits," December 22, 1976.

Cape Cod Times. "Liberian Tanker Grounds on Nantucket Shoals," December 15, 1976, p. 1.

———. "Specialists Join CG in Battle against Spillage," December 16, 1976, p. 1.

———. "Tanker Evacuated," December 17, 1976, p. 1.

———. "Abandoned Tanker 'Belching' Thick Oil," December 18, 1976, p. 1.

———. "Oil Leak Now 1.5M Gallons," December 20, 1976, p. 1.

———. "Rough Seas Smash Tanker in Half," December 21, 1976, p. 1.

———. "Oil Threat to Bank Ebbs," December 24, 1976, p. 1.

———. "Oil Stalls Off Nantucket," December 27, 1976, p. 1.

———. "Oil Slick Stretches 141 Miles; Heads Out to Sea," December 28, 1976, p. 1.

Winslow, Ron. *Hard Aground.* New York: W.W. Norton & Company, 1978.

WIND, WAVES, AND SNOW
The Great Whiteout (1978)

Boston Evening Globe. "Brace Yourself!," February 6, 1978, p. 1.

Boston Globe. "Blizzard Batters New England," February 7, 1978, p. 1.

———. "Worst Storm of Century," February 8, 1978.

———. "Punchy N.E. Fights Back," February 9, 1978, p. 1.

Boston Herald American. "Here We Go Again: Heavy Snow Sweeping toward N.E.," February 6, 1978, p. 1.

———. "Another Real Whipping," February 7, 1978, p. 1.

———. "Blizzard '78," February 8, 1978.

———. "U.S. Troops to the Rescue!" February 9, 1978.

———. "We Still Have a Long Way to Go," February 10, 1978.

———. "Carter Approves Disaster Funds—Driving Ban Still On," February 11, 1978.

Lawrence Eagle-Tribune. "Wow What a Blow!" February 7, 1978, p. 1.

———. "It's Over," February 8, 1978.

UNDERGROUND MIRACLE
Collision at Back Bay Station (1990)

Boston Globe. "280 Hurt in Back Bay Rail Crash," December 13,
　　1990.
———. "Brake Failure Is Called Cause of Crash," December 14,
　　1990, p. 1.
Boston Herald. "Rookie on the Rails," December 13, 1990.
———. "Train Boss Had Bad Track Record," December 14, 1990,
　　p. 1.
National Transportation Safety Board. *Response to Petition for
　　Reconsideration.* File MC980669, Accident DCA91MR003,
　　December 15, 1999.

About the Author

LARRY PLETCHER has investigated the natural treasures and history of New England for nearly thirty years. After graduating from Princeton University and receiving an advanced degree from UCLA, Larry returned East and combined a professional career with freelance writing, photography, and avid exploration. A resident of Warner, New Hampshire, where he lives with his wife and daughter, Larry has called an old New England farmhouse home since 1975. He is the author of *It Happened in Massachusetts* and several outdoor recreation guides.